A TRUE STORY

IOWA HILL

Gold, Guns, Guts, and God

Jim Bean

Nampa, Idaho

ISBN: 978-1-7333468-2-5

Library of Congress Number: 2024908512

United in Christ
Ministries LLC

I dedicate this book to all the old miners that spent their life looking for gold.

To my grandfather, who worked in the deep mines and died of miners' consumption.

To Mike Wartburg, for our years of mining together. This book would not have been possible if it wasn't for him, his love for mining, and his time spent in this adventure with me.

To miners Benny and Frank, brothers. I was blessed to be able to spend time with them on the American River, at their claim.

To all of the people I got to know and make friends with during my time in Iowa Hill. I will never forget them.

And to my wife, Kristina, of 41 years of marriage, whom I would not have met if it wasn't for this mine that I opened. She is a gift from God who changed my life forever.

God bless them all!

CONTENTS

INTRODUCTION

We were gold miners. This is a true story about opening a gold mine that had been closed for almost a half a century. It was an opportunity to go back in time and experience what it was like. It was given to me by a man that was haunted by his experience in the mine a long time ago and his obsession to open it one more time. That's what this story is all about and what it was like to do that.

Let me tell you about the town of Iowa Hill. It was originally called Iowa City in 1852. Rich diggings were discovered at Iowa Hill in 1853. The town sprang up from one tent store and three log cabins to a town with the usual array of saloons, gambling houses, hotels, butcher shops, provision stores, dry goods, and clothing stores. It also had a bowling alley, a theater, an ice cream parlor and two churches. Iowa Hill was sometimes called Magic Town due to its rapid growth. The population totaled between 1,400 and 1,600 people in 1854. It was a roaring mining camp with bull and bear fights, held on Sugarloaf Mountain, overlooking Iowa Hill. Gambling and, unfortunately, one lynching occurred in an effort to bring stability.

The Mountain Blues, one of the first state regulated Militia, in Placer County, was formed there. In July 1855 (as surface gold was depleted in 1875), the miners of Iowa Hill dug into the ancient channels that entered through the Iowa Hill divide. It was a hard life. Some found gold; others failed. Many miners are buried in the old Iowa Hill cemetery. If you visit the Iowa Hill Cemetery, put a flower on a grave.

CHAPTER ONE

It was the early spring of 1980. I was 40 years old working for a company in the Napa Valley, California region. I had been working for them since I was 16 years old. The man that owned the company was not only my boss, but he was also my friend. My dad had worked for this same place for several years, too, as a supervisor. In 1962, he had a heart attack on one of his jobs and 10 days later passed away. I was 22 years old at that time and over the years that followed, my boss treated me like family. I always had a job. I was married early in life at the age of 20 and after my dad died, my wife and I had two children. I had been married for 19 years when things started to go south in our marriage which would lead to a divorce.

I had been living in a 16-foot travel trailer for about a year and a half at Springs Street RV Park in Vallejo, California. I just didn't care about anything. I felt betrayed, and I wasn't taking care of myself—working hard to take my mind off of reality and eating junk food. I missed a stable family, I was lonely, and I was living like a bum and didn't care.

I guess my boss was seeing what was going on. He came to me one day and said, "How would you like to go gold mining? I have an old mine that I own. It has been in the back of my mind for several years now. I last had it open in the 1940s. All these years, it has been sitting there since I first opened it up. Nobody's been there since I closed it down and blew up the portal entrance."

I lit up like a kid in a candy store. My answer was a big, "Yes, when do we get started?"

He told me to, "Get ready, and I will let you know."

My family had a lot of mining experience. My grandfather had worked in the deep gold mines in Nevada City and Grass Valley area and numerous other mines in Northern California.

He had died of miners' consumption. It was a lung disease that you would receive from quartz dust working underground. My dad and my uncles were miners and loggers, so I grew up learning about how to mine. I actually had worked in a mine that my dad had when I was going to high school, it was on our property. We lived on Bean Road in Auburn, California. I did dredging in the rivers in the summer and had learned how to pan for gold—there is a correct way of doing that. I was familiar with underground mining. I had the best experience with good teachers. That is why I was so excited about going.

This mine was about 150 miles from the Napa Valley, away from all of my problems. I was having a terrible time getting along with my ex-wife, and she was giving me a difficult time seeing my kids. I was hoping that going out of town would give me a chance to clear my head.

About two days later, in the morning, my boss drove up in his white Suburban, the tinted window rolled down. He said, "Get in the car. We're going up to the mine." So, I got in and off we went to see this old mine back in the hills. About three hours later, we pulled off the main paved road onto an old dirt road. We started down through some brush, potholes, trees, and lots of rock piles as the road grew narrow. I noticed a ridge with a vertical cliff on both sides. I guess the best word is remote, very remote.

After some time, we came to a wide spot in the road. He stopped and said, "We're here."

It looked like we landed in a brush patch, with the brush over my head and tons of rocks and trees. There was a cliff over 200 feet straight up and nothing recognizable. I couldn't make heads or tails out of what I was seeing. It's funny how you can think of something totally different in your mind. I looked at him and said, "This looks like someplace you would never find your way out of." We got out of the car and walked around.

He said, "I think they had a tunnel someplace there," and pointed to the 200-foot cliff. It all looked the same to me.

I was thinking, *What did I get myself into?*

My boss looked at me and said, "When we get back to the office, go by the shop and get a chainsaw and whatever you need to make a place for your trailer. Let me know if you need anything else to get this mine going."

I said, "Okay," but was thinking, *What mine?* on the way out of this remote dust-eaten road.

We stopped for dinner on our way to Vallejo. That's when he elaborated to me about what happened at the old mine in the 1940s. He had a man running it, one that he trusted. My boss was trying to get his contracting business going in Vallejo, California at the same time, so he wasn't able to travel back and forth to check on things.

One weekend my boss's sister and her husband were in Forest Hill having dinner. There was a man there who had been drinking, bragging about the gold he was finding in a mine. He was happy to show them and had them come outside as he fumbled for the keys to open up the trunk of his car. There he had several dozen monster-sized fruit jars that were filled to the brim with nuggets of gold. In his drunken stupor, he named the mine, and it just happened to be the one my boss owned. He was stealing gold from my boss!

Stunned by the information they heard and seeing the jars of gold nuggets, his sister and brother-in-law raced back to Vallejo and told him all about what they had heard. He was furious and believed the information that his sister reported to him. He drove up and shut down the mine. He said he sent the man walking out with no vehicle and then blew up the entrance to the tunnel.

After 40 years, it would be difficult to find the entrance with all the brush and trees. Now I had a full understanding of what I was looking at. I was excited at the challenge knowing that I could find the tunnel. I now realized that my job was to find it, open it, and make it work. All the way back home, my boss put great faith in me knowing that I could do the job. I didn't want to let him down.

CHAPTER TWO

I had no idea what I was going to do first. I had so many things spinning around in my mind, so I slept on it that night. I got up the next morning excited about my new adventure, walked around my trailer, unplugged the electricity and water, drained all the tanks, and hooked it up to my truck. I stopped by my house, told my ex and my kids that I was taking a job out of town. The only one that was sad to see me go was my son. As I drove away, I looked in the rearview mirror and saw him crying. It made me sad but, at the same time, I knew I had to do something to get my head clear and not do something stupid because of my anger toward her.

After several hours of driving, I pulled up in the brush patch, got out and looked around. It was quiet as a graveyard. I grabbed the chainsaw and went to work cutting down trees and brush, working on a spot for my new home and wondered how long I would be there. The sun was going down, and the night would be on me soon. I left the trailer hooked up to the truck and went to bed. I would back it up in my spot that I cleared the next day.

I did not sleep much that night. My mind would not stop thinking about my new adventure, my kids, and how it came to this. The next morning, I stumbled out of the trailer and looked around at my new home. The birds were my only companions.

After a time walking around and surveying the area, I realized that back during the gold rush, they used water cannons to wash down the mountains. I'm looking at a 200-foot vertical cliff. This had to be one of those mines, an ancient river channel of cemented gravel. The only way to get in now would be a tunnel in, and that is what they had done. They had shut off hydraulic mining in the earlier days because it was washing mud into the rivers and polluting them, plus it was destroying the land. This 200-foot cliff told me this is where the old timers stopped with their water cannons. In order to get anything else, we would need to enter in. I would have to tunnel into the mountain or find the old tunnel that my boss caved in years back.

The next morning, I got up and backed my truck and trailer into the spot that I had cleared the day before. I unhooked it and set it up for the long-haul not knowing how much time I would be there. I got out my notebook and started to write things down that I would need to get started, then I would call my boss and give him my order. That afternoon, I went out to get a hold of him.

My mom lived in Auburn, about 35 miles away. I would stay there overnight, have a nice meal, a shower, and a good night's sleep and go to Vallejo the next morning. I decided I wanted to talk to my boss instead of calling him. My mom was happy that I would be closer, and that I would be stopping there from time to time but was sad for the split up and grandkids being so far away.

The next morning, I left early. I got down to the office and went in to see my boss. He was happy to see me. I gave him my list: a backhoe, fuel tank, generator for my trailer, and a 50-gallon water tank for my trailer, some tools, and a truck to use. He would send it and some other things he thought I would need. He said he would have the list on its way in two days. I went back up to the mine to do some more work on clearing out the brush and trees for a place to park my truck.

I spent the rest of the day walking back and forth at the face of the cliff looking for something that looked like a cave in. About 100 feet away from my trailer was a dent in the bank. I thought that may be the best place to start. My boss was sending me the backhoe I had requested, so I could dig back in once I located a spot. I decided that would be the first place that I would start to dig.

About that time, I was getting hungry and realized I didn't get any food to eat so it was crackers and peanut butter for dinner that night. Old Mother Hubbard's cupboards were bare in the trailer. I think the peanut butter was from the house when I left and the crackers were old. I remembered a man telling me that there was a store about seven miles from the mine on the old road to the city of Colfax. I had not been on that road, but I knew where it was.

The next day at 11 o'clock, my stomach was growling, so I took off to find that store. It was a terrible little narrow road but after a time, I came into Iowa Hill and there it was, a little store. It had two front doors next to each other. I parked in front and went in the first door.

A man inside stood 5'8" and was about 140 pounds and in his late 50s. He said, "What can I do for you? This is the post office." I looked around the corner, and there were a few cans of food to buy.

I told him I was hungry, and he let me know that next door was the bar and they could make me a hamburger. That sounded great to me. I went out that door and into the next door. Inside were a few chairs, an old pool table, and six or seven old men sitting in the chairs giving me the evil eye. I went up to the bar and ordered a hamburger and a cold beer.

All the time, they kept staring at me. Then one of them asked, "What are you doing here?"

"Just passing through," I assured them.

Another one on the other side spoke a harsh, "Good!"

I wolfed down my hamburger, drank my beer, paid the bill, and got out of there.

The next day, the truck with the backhoe and other things I had ordered came in. They gave me an old pickup truck that was decent and a gas card. They had a 500-gallon fuel tank with diesel in it for the backhoe. I also received a message to call my boss. I thanked the crew who delivered it all before they left.

It was late, so I decided I would go to my mom's house, get some food for the week, and call my boss. I also decided to go to the sheriff's office and get a blasting permit. I had a license, but I would need a blasting permit to buy dynamite. I had gone to school with the sheriff, so I sat down and told him my plans at the mine.

That's when he said, "Get a shotgun and a mean dog. We only go in there with a S.W.A.T. team." At first, I thought he was kidding, but no one laughed when he said it. On the way out he said, "If you have to shoot someone, call us, and we will come get the body."

As I left his office, I thought, *What was that all about?* I went ahead and called my boss who informed me he would be up in about a week. I bought some groceries for the week. I knew that he would be wanting to see my progress, so I started back to the mine.

I decided to travel in from a different way—through Colfax. As I went down the road, it was very narrow and windy. Now I knew why they told me to go in from the Forest Hill side, as you could not make the turns with a large truck much bigger than a pickup truck.

As I made my way down to the river and across the bridge, I started up the other side. I saw a man—a big man—limping as he walked up the road. He was about 250 pounds, around 6'2" and he had dark hair with an old tee shirt and cut-off jeans. I stopped and asked him if I could help him.

He looked at me and said, "Do you have a first-aid kit?"

I told him I did and pulled over and got out of my truck with the first-aid kit. He pointed at his ankle. There was blood coming out on both sides of it. He said it was a bullet hole. It had gone clear through but had not hit the bone. I was shocked. I poured alcohol in one side, and it came out the other. I

bandaged him up the best I could. He asked me if I would give him a ride up the hill. I said, "Sure," and he got into my truck.

All the way up the hill, he never said a word until we reached the top. "Drop me off on the other side of the store, and I will walk into my camp." I offered to take him to the hospital, but he would have nothing to do with that.

I put away my groceries and some tools that I had purchased— a little iron table and a lounge chair for sitting outside. I piled some rocks in a circle for a campfire. After that, I went in and made dinner. Then, after some time, I went to bed. It was hard for me to sleep. I thought about what the sheriff had said to me about this place. I would hear every crack or noise in the brush and birds that would make noises most of the night.

The next morning, I ate a little cereal, got dressed, and went outside early in the morning. The smells from the pine trees were wonderful before the sun came up. I went over to the backhoe and started it up to let it warm up. I would start digging in the dent that I had seen at the base of the 200-foot cliff, about 100 feet from my trailer.

After about two hours digging in the bank, I saw some dirt falling and a black hole was revealed. *Was this the tunnel?* I was excited that I had made some progress. I stopped for a fast lunch and to get a flashlight out of the trailer that I had kept for emergencies and took off to the black hole.

I cleared around the hole, removed more dirt out of the way so I could look in. It was a tunnel, not a very big tunnel. It looked to be about five feet high. I got the backhoe and cleared all the dirt away from the opening to where I could go in and look around. I was amazed that it was so small—about two and a half feet wide, five feet high.

I bent way down and walked in about 20 feet when my flashlight went out. Of course, it would be just like the old thriller movies. The batteries were old, and I had none in the trailer. How could I forget batteries to have a light to go into a tunnel? I went back to the trailer sat down in my new chair thinking, *If I'm going to do this, I need to get a scratch pad and start writing down things that I need that I keep forgetting about.* I didn't know what to do. Then I thought, *Why couldn't I get a stick, dip it in diesel fuel, and make a torch to go in the mine and look around.* So, I did. I lit it and started back in with my torch. About 50 feet into the tunnel, it made a left turn. I followed it in for about 70 feet and it came into a huge room, full of water, which was leaning and headed toward the outside wall. That must be where the old tunnel came in.

About that time, my torch started going out and my head started to hurt. At that moment, I realized I was in bad air. There is bad air in all mines that have been condemned; it is very dangerous. There was a lack of oxygen. I had to get out of there immediately or risk dying. I had been too excited and wasn't thinking, and I knew better. I've been around mines all my life. The old miners called it white damp, kind of like hydrogen sulfide, a deadly gas. With all my excitement, I was not paying attention to what I had learned. I realized if I was going to live and work in this mine I would have to start using my head. That was a close call. From then on, it would be safety first.

I sat down and started to draw a diagram of what I had seen. Then I went and got a 100-foot tape and measured across the face of the bluff from where I saw that room of water and where it might have come out. That would be the next spot where I would dig the next hole into the bank the next day.

I started digging in that spot and broke into a big tunnel above the water that was caved in, I would need a bigger backhoe to reach farther into the tunnel to get the mud out. You could look inside the tunnel and see the huge body of water.

I went out and made a phone call. My boss said he would send me a bigger backhoe and would send his son up with a pump for water and a cat loader to help move dirt. He told me not to leave the mine. I didn't tell him I was already in town. I was going to my mom's house to pick up my handgun and to stop at the gun shop to purchase a seven-shot pump shotgun and two boxes of buckshot.

I headed back toward the mine. I went in the same way I had earlier in the week on the crooked road after I crossed the bridge down at the river and started up the other side about two miles. Someone shot a hole in my windshield as I was driving. I was pretty shaken over that! The sheriff's words rang through my head again. *Get a shotgun and a mean dog.* Luckily, no one was riding with me or they might've been killed.

When I got back to the mine, I put a piece of tape over the hole and cleaned the glass out of my truck. After some time (and a stiff drink), I was ready to find out what kind of nuthouse surrounded me. I was raised by tough men in my life, so I went to the only place that had been here for 100 years—the Iowa Hill Post Office Bar and Grocery Store combo. I parked in front of the bar, walked in with my shotgun, and sidearm strapped to my leg like I owned the place.

The first person to talk to me was Moe, the owner. "What can I get for you?"

I worked my way around the bar and put my back up against the wall. There was about six grubby men sitting around. I said, "I want to know who the bull of the woods is—the number one dude on this damn hill." Shock was on their faces. I continued, "Someone put a bullet hole in my windshield, and I want some answers."

Moe was trying to calm me down, but that wasn't working. One of the men raised his arm and said, "That would be King Kup. He lives down by the river. The old road just out of town goes to his camp. If I were you, I wouldn't go there. You might not come back."

I told him I gave a tall man a ride and let him out at that road the other day.

"You're the one that helped him?" one asked. When I told him I was, he said, "That was Kup. We heard about it from TomTom, the Indian."

"Who is that?" I asked.

"He is part of Kup's family down there."

I asked, "How many are down in Kup's camp?"

"A lot," was the answer.

I shook Moe's hand and told him that we were starting a little mine and I would talk to him later as I would be looking for three or four men to work for me that lived on the hill.

He replied, "Just let me know."

I went back to the mine, ate dinner and went to bed.

The next day, the truck came in with the big backhoe. The truck driver that brought in the backhoe told me another truck had dropped off a cat loader, and a man was driving it into the mine, and that the man would go back with him to Vallejo afterward. Well, after some time, I was wondering where he was. We jumped in my truck and went looking for him. About two miles up the road, we saw a man in the road waving at us. Something was wrong. When we got to him, he was moaning in pain. He had lost his brakes, and when the loader started to go over the bank, he jumped and broke his leg.

I looked over the bank and down the hill and up against a tree was my loader. The truck driver that was with me would have to walk the two miles back to the mine as I was at full speed going to the Auburn Hospital. At the hospital, after I knew he was in good hands, I called the office and told them what happened so that they could notify his family, then I called my boss. He was not happy and felt bad. Someone had sent the wrong loader. He would take care of it. He asked me what it would take to get the loader back up on the road. I told him some big cables and a D8 cat bulldozer, He made a list and told me that his son would be up with a transport hauling the bulldozer the next morning, so I went back down to the mine. I thanked God that the man was going to be fine, but he could've been killed just as easy.

I had some time to kill, so I took a little ride. I knew the name of the old mine, and I wondered how many old timers with the same name worked there years past. I drove up to the old cemetery and walked around looking at some of the old tombstones with the same name as the mine. I was amazed how many old miners worked there in years past.

That night, I had a dream about something I should do, and I decided I would do it, but it would have to wait until we got the loader back up on the road the next day. The truck came in with the bulldozer and with Denny, the boss's son, with the big cables. There was a pine tree up across the road from the loader over the bank. We would put a big clevis around the tree and run a huge cable from the bulldozer through the clevis then down to the loader over the bank to pull it out. We pulled it back up on the road and loaded it on the transport to go back to

Vallejo. I drove the bulldozer down to the mine and helped Denny get his truck unloaded so he could go home. I went to bed and slept for about ten hours.

It was Sunday morning. I went to see my mom. When I got there, I told her what this little voice told me to do in my dream. I was to put flowers on the names of all the graves that had anything to do with that mine. My mom agreed and went along with me, so we picked a ton of flowers around the house. I loaded her in the truck, and we headed up to the Iowa Hill Cemetery. We put flowers on all of the tombstones that had the name of Gleason. The last headstone caught my attention because it said, "As you are now, I once was. As I am now, you soon will be; so as you walk by, pray for me."

CHAPTER THREE

I took Mom home and went back to the mine. When I got there, there were two men waiting for me. They said they were sent up to run the big backhoe. I told them we would start in the morning.

The next morning, I told them that there was a spot I had picked out where we would start digging. About four hours in, we had cleaned out the old tunnel entrance; it was full of water, and it was deep. I paid them for all day and their trip up and back and sent them home. I had found the old mine entrance. Now it was up to the man paying the bills to designate what to do next. He would have to come up and decide.

The rest of the day I did clean up with the bulldozer and made a place for my pickup and a spot to put my water tank and generator next to my trailer. I would have to haul my water to my tank whenever I was around a fresh water source. The water at the mine wasn't good for drinking or for a shower. There was a creek about three miles away that ran under the road. There was a large culvert pipe where the water would fall like a shower. I would park my truck out of sight and take my clothes off. Then with a bar of soap, I would shower. It was darn cold, but it worked. No one noticed me from the road.

It was around noon, and I was having some lunch when I heard someone coming down the ridge. I looked outside my window. A big van and a pickup truck was in front of my trailer. It was my boss, his wife, and son, and a man that I knew, and his wife. I went out to greet them. They were all looking around at all the work I had done. They wanted to see the entrance into the mine, and they were interested in the story of how I found it. I sat down and told them the whole story of how I found an old Chinese tunnel and that led me to walk in and find where the other tunnel entered the mountain. Then Tony, my boss, told me that my old friend, Mike, would work for me. Mike and Denny went to school together and were buddies.

I was thinking, *I can see the writing on the wall; he would be their spy to keep watch over me.* Mike lived about 30 miles away and would drive back and forth from his house. You would have to be a nut to drive back and forth on that road, but I looked at Mike and said, "Great! Welcome to the mine. We will have a lot to talk about. When can you start?"

He smiled and said, "Tomorrow."

We all walked over to the main entrance. They got a little too close. I told them, "Stand back. If even a little rock rolls down that hill for 200 feet and hits you in the head, you'll be dead." I informed Tony that we needed something to put in front of the tunnel. He came up with the idea to put two huge pipes, six feet high and fifteen feet long, at the entrance of the tunnel which would make it safe from falling rock. We planned to go in and pump out the water. He would send me a bigger pump the following day along with some 20-pound track and two mine cars. He told me he was building a gold recovery plant and would start sending equipment and people to put it together. I was thinking that now all these things and people would make me more responsible. My boss went back home, leaving me with a lot on my mind.

CHAPTER FOUR

I had Mike and his wife stay so we could have a little talk. I was straightforward with him. If he was going to watch my back underground, I would have to be able to trust him so I asked him, "Are you a spy for the old man, or are you here to work?"

He raised his voice and looked me in the eyes and said that he was there to work then stated, "I need a job closer to home."

"Well then, come in tomorrow and we'll get started." I told him to pack a gun and shared what had happened to me. I told Mike he would be the mine foreman and would help me make this whole situation work, outside and underground, and to do it safely. I made sure he knew I was glad to have him. His wife gave me a hug, and they left to go home.

I took a drive up to the Iowa Hill store and went into the bar to see if Moe had found some workers for me. And there he was—Kup—the man I had helped with a bullet hole in his leg.

I walked over to him. "So, you're Kup."

He looked at me, got up, and said, "King of."

"I would like to come down to your camp tomorrow and talk to you."

He looked at me and smiled and said, "Just you. No one else."

I simply answered, "Okay. See you around noon."

Moe followed me out and said, "I will send two men down in a couple of days that are looking for a job." I let him know I would talk with them. Moe added, "Are you sure you want to go to Kup's camp?"

I said, "Moe, I want four cases of beer, three or four bottles of wine, and I will pick them up at 11 o'clock in the morning."

The look on his face was something else, and he said, "Okay."

I went back to the mine and made a list of things to do and then sat down in my lounge chair wondering what this place was going to look like in a month. I cleaned up my trailer and was wondering if I could build a little building, maybe twelve feet by 8 feet, which would fit on my trailer to have a wood stove in so I could open my door and let some heat in this winter.

The next day, Mike came at six in the morning ready to go to work. I told him about the shed and asked him to make a list of things he would need to build it and to go grab the materials. I informed him I would be going to Kup's camp. He went to his truck and got his gun and said, "I'm going with you."

I told him, "No. I gave him my word that I would come alone."

Mike wasn't happy with me and said, "I will come after you if you aren't here in the morning."

With a smile, I said, "That works." He took off to get the wood for our shed afterward.

I went and got some money and went up to the store to get my order from Moe. When I got to the store, Moe had it all ready for me, and we put it in my truck. He told me two men would be coming to the job site.

I told him that would be fine and took off for Kup's camp about a mile out of town. I turned down an old dirt road past a "No Trespassing" sign and then a "Turn Back" sign past the "You will be Shot" sign. I came to a small campground of about ten people. I stopped, rolled down the window and asked, "Is this Kup's camp? They pointed down the road, and they started walking down behind me as I drove through some brush and came out in a clearing.

There was an old house and some out buildings that looked to have been abandoned at one time. When I came to the front of the house, I stopped. Several men surrounded the truck. I opened up the door and got out and looked around. I said, "I'm here to see King Kup."

About that time, he came out of the old house with no shirt on, cut-off jeans, and barefooted. In his hand, he had a big machete. He laid it down and said, "Welcome to my world."

Boy, was I relieved! I shook his hand and told him that I had a gift for the camp in the back of my truck. He looked in the back of my truck at the several cases of beer and wine. He then reached for the latch on my tailgate, opened it, and sat on it.

He opened a beer for himself and one for me and said, "Okay, let me introduce you to my family." First, he pointed to a man probably in his 20s. "This is little Kup." He was about five eight and a handsome man. He looked to be in good shape. Kup said, "He is my brother and my lieutenant. This other man, standing over here is Tom-Tom."

I looked at him. He was heavyset and looked grubby. He said he was an Indian. He dressed like an Indian. He had a knife in his belt and looked mean. He was definitely somebody you wouldn't want to fight with. He came over and shook my hand. His deep and broken language reminded me of something I would hear on the movie set of the Lone Ranger. "You have guts to be here."

Kup pointed at an old man who was extremely skinny with rotten teeth. He was dressed in black with a big black hat on his head. He said, "I'm Pappy Kup,"

My opinion was that he was a dirty old man with a bad mouth, every other word was a cuss word. About that time, the door to the house opened and out stepped a woman that, to me, looked pregnant. She had brown hair, and she was not very big—about five six. She said, "Hello." Behind her, I noticed three or four small children and a girl that looked to be about 15 years old.

Kup said, "This is my woman." He walked over and pulled up her blouse and said, "She has nice erasers."

I looked the other way as she pulled her blouse back down and looked at me and said, "My name is Feather."

"Nice to meet you," I replied.

I looked around and counted probably 30 people around the truck. I told Kup that I was going to run a mine over the mountain and I didn't want any trouble. He asked me where it was, and I told him.

He had Tom Tom unload what was left in the back of my truck, opened another can of beer, and said, "You will have no problem with us. What we do is our business. What you do is your business. I will have respect for our friendship. There are others on the mountain that I am not responsible for, but if you have a problem, come to me."

I told him if I saw any of them walking in or out, they were to flag me down for a ride. It was getting late, so I said goodbye to them with a good attitude about what we had talked about. I went back to the mine, ate some cereal, and went to sleep.

CHAPTER FIVE

The next morning, Mike came in with some lumber, plywood, two by fours, and an old wood stove, and some stove pipe. That was a surprise. We spent the day putting the shed together. I told him that we had a truce with Kup the King of. He laughed and said, "I will abide by it."

I told him that men and trucks would be coming in tomorrow, so he would need to get some rest when he got home. He had a tendency to let people come over and party all night. I needed him rested up and ready to go to work the next day. I went to bed early, as well, but was not able to sleep much thinking about the next day. Finally, I got up about five in the morning. I made some coffee. It was chilly, so I made a fire in my new stove. At first, it smoked up my trailer. I had to open up the shed door, all the time wondering if this was a good idea. It finally stopped smoking, and I could feel the heat.

I put my chair in front of the stove, sat back and fell asleep, only to wake up with Mike pounding at the door. "Wake up! A truck is coming down the hill. It's time to rock and roll."

I pulled my boots on and went outside. The truck came in loaded down with a big generator, a compressor for air for the mine, and the drills that would be used in the mine for drilling. The truck behind him was carrying a new loader. A powder magazine is about the size of a small camper made out of steel for explosives, and there was a van to store our tools and equipment. More trucks came in with the gold-washing plant; it would have to be put together. Then came the big pipes to go into the entrance of the mine. There were men to help plus the mechanics from Vallejo to help put it all together. It was busy all day, getting things unloaded and put in their place.

We would start pumping water out of the mine first. We had to drain it so we could lay down the track for the mining cars. We would start pumping water out of the mine the following day. We cleared out a spot to slide the pipe in the entrance going into the tunnel. With that finished, we were ready to pump the water out that afternoon.

Two men came in—Randy and John. They wanted a job as laborers. I told them I would start them at $200 a week for 40 hours and informed them that they had to get some boots and gloves. If they did that, they could start the next day.

By the next week, we would have a full crew, some from Vallejo. Mike, Randy, John, and I would be stretching electric cables to the plant, placing pipes for the water on the plant for washing the rocks. We would make a pond for water and pump water out of the tunnel in the morning into the pond. When the pond was full, we would recycle that water to run the plant.

The plant consisted of a big hopper in front with a grizzly on top of it. The grizzly consisted of bars that were across the top of the hopper to keep the bigger rocks from going into the plant. The loader would dump the dirt on top of it to separate the dirt from the boulders. The washing plant was a pipe about five feet in diameter, twenty-five feet long with three-quarter inch punch holes in the end of it that rotated. The water was pumped in to wash the dirt as the pipe rotated. The gold would fall through the punch holes into the sluice boxes. There was a stacker belt that went out the end of the pipe to carry the oversized rocks out and onto a dump. The water would go through the wash plant, which was the long pipe with the holes, washing with the trommel turning. The bigger rocks that went through the grizzly would fall inside and were crushed, the smaller rocks and dirt would go down into the sluice boxes which consisted of two 40-foot-long sluice boxes with ruffles in them to catch the gold. The water would go back into the pond. After a week of putting everything together, we were ready to go mining.

CHAPTER SIX

We started one morning putting the track rails down the slope going into the mine floor. Laying down the track rails is a job in itself. You must support the rails or else it would just fall over in the mud. The rails were similar to railroad track supported with wood and large rail nail pegs. Each rail was twelve feet long. We had pumped out all the water into the pond, and it was full.

With the ramp coming out of the mine, we would have to build an extension out of wood the same level as the mine floor to take the ore, which was the dirt, up on the elevated platform. There, we would dump the mine cars. When we brought the mine cars out of the mine, we would have an air-driven winch at the top of the ramp and a cable to pull the mine cars up that ramp to dump them. We built a rail stop so the mine car would not go off the track. The loader would pick the dirt up where we had dumped it and put it through the plant. With that all installed, we were ready to go.

We took a break the rest of the day, built a fire in the fire pit I had made, got out some beer, and sat there celebrating late into the night—Mike, John, Randy, and I. I wanted to know something about the people that I had hired to work in the mine. Randy and John were from Iowa Hill. Mike was from Grass Valley.

Randy and John had lit up a couple of marijuana cigarettes. I told them I did not care what they did on their time, but they were never to do that on my time in this mine. If they did, they would be gone. I knew then that hiring men out of the woods could be a problem. They left to go home. Mike slept in his truck, and I went to bed.

The next morning, I got up around 6 a.m. and made some breakfast. I went out and woke Mike up and told him to come in and eat something before we went to work. John and Randy came in at eight that day. We installed an air line in the mine for the drills and put up some timbers to start the tunnel. I decided which way we were going to go. We got our hardhats with the carbide lamps that were attached to the front of the hardhat. They were powered by the reaction of calcium carbonate, Ca C2, with water (H2O). This reaction produces acetylene gas, C2 H2, which burns a clean white flame. The 49er miners used candles then along came these lights later. We would get electric ones several months later.

Mike and I went in and looked around a big room with a cemented gravel pillar in the middle of it to hold the roof up. They had taken a lot out of this area. This must've been where Tony and the man hired worked when he was kicked out of the mine in the 1940s.

An ancient underground river channel is just like any other river channel except it's underground. At one time, it was on top of the ground, but then it was covered up with volcanic action, and turned into cemented gravel. I would have to follow the blue bedrock to find the gold and, with doing that, I would have to drill a tunnel into it and use explosives. I would set up a hydraulic Jack Leg to raise the drill up in the air to support the jackhammer which weighed about 125 pounds, with a six-foot steel drill at the end of it. The jackhammer drill would hammer a six-foot hole back in the face of the wall. There would be nine holes drilled, three at the top, three at the center, and three at the bottom, which we called lifters. We would bring rail track up to two feet of the face then put an aluminum plate down on the floor to make it easier for the miner to dig or shovel off into the mine car.

After everything was ready to go, I needed to travel to the town of Lincoln to get some hard sticks of 40-percent dynamite, which we called powder. We got six boxes; the rest would come in from a different company with the caps and fuses. I headed back to the mine and put the dynamite into one of the powder magazines and the caps and fused in another powder magazine. You never store them together.

We started up everything to see if we were ready. I sat down with the crew and I talked about safety concerns for each job running the plant and what our responsibilities would be. I asked if they had any questions. We would start in the morning at 8 a.m. sharp, and I warned them not to be late. Now the responsibility for my men and their safety was up to me.

The night went by fast, but there was not much sleep. Everyone was on time the next morning. I gave Randy and John some work outside to do. Then Mike and I packed the drill into the mine. We hooked it up to the air hose and a small water hose that would send water to the drill steel, which went into the drill hole to keep the dust down before we would start to drill. We looked over the roof in the tunnel to see if there were any cracks or loose rock that would fall down. If we saw what we thought would fall on us, we would take a long steel bar and knock down any loose rock.

Now we were ready to start drilling. We would lift the drill with the help of the jack that went from the back of the drill to the tunnel floor and point the steel in the direction we wanted to go and start drilling. Holding the jackhammer up, even though you have support of the leg on the ground floor, isn't easy. The hammer is extremely loud, heavy, and it vibrates. With a good jackhammer, it takes about 20 minutes to drill one hole.

You drill first the center hole, then a hole to the left and to the right that would be the center of the tunnel. Then you drill three above and three below. That would make a tunnel about six feet high and five feet wide. We finished drilling the holes, so we were ready to load the holes with dynamite.

Mike and I went out to have some lunch. I was not happy with the drill. It was old and slow. We were supposed to get a new one after lunch. We went down to the powder magazine, got the powder for the shot, and then to a smaller magazine some distance away for the fuse and caps. We then came back to the tunnel to load the holes. The holes were drilled six feet in depth. We took a stick of dynamite and poked a hole in the end of it about the size of a quarter inch with a round wooden stick. Then a copper cap about an inch and a half long filled with explosives (the detonator to set the dynamite off) was placed about a half inch into the dynamite. There was a hole in the end of the copper cap. The fuse would then be slid into the hole of the copper cap then crimped around the fuse.

The old miners would usually use their teeth to crimp it. (That was not a good idea.) We used a crimping tool. With the fuse inserted into the cap then into the dynamite, we were ready to put it in the hole. With three or four extra sticks of dynamite, we would tamp them in with a long wooden pole. The fuse altogether would be over seven and a half feet long. That would give us about a foot and a half outside of the hole to light it and give us time to light all nine holes and get out of the tunnel.

With the fuse outside of the holes, we would take the end of the fuse and cut a small diagonal hole in the end of it about one inch back that would expose the powder and make it easier to light with our gas lamps or a match. We would light the center hole then the one to the left of it and to the right of it. Then we would go up and light the center hole on top and the one to the left of it and the right of it. Lastly, we would go down to the lifters at the bottom of the tunnel, light the center one and the one on the left and the one on the right. With all of them lit, it was time to get out of the tunnel. You would then yell "Fire in the hole!"

Lighting them by hand, from fuse to fuse, would give you a little time from hole to hole, so you would count them when they went off to make sure that they all did, for safety's sake. They all went off; the shot was successful. We waited for the smoke to clear to go back in to see our first shot; it was good. We would muck it out in the morning into the mine cars then take it outside and dump it off the ramp. We would pick it up with a loader and put it in the plant. We started mining the next morning. At that moment, we were an operational mine.

The next morning, I got up early to start the water pump in the tunnel to drain it before we started to work. It was a beautiful day. The men all came in, and we started the plant which consisted of starting the generator and the compressor. I also started up the D8 cat.

Mike and John and Randy were all on time, I sent them in the mine to load the mine cars. Then I went over to get the D8 cat. There was a mound off of the tunnel that looked to me like the miners had left it. I took the cat with rippers on the back and ripped it up. I would pile it up to run it through the plant. There was gold in it, but the problem was it made too much mud.

Just as I finished piling it up, I noticed a car coming into the mine. It was Tony and his son, Denny. There was another man in the car that I'd never seen before. I was surprised that they came in on the day we would start running the plant. I was hoping that they wouldn't come in until we got all the bugs worked out, but there they were.

I walked over and shook the hand of my boss, and he introduced me to the new man, Charles. He told me that this man was familiar with the mine and had something to do with it with him. He never told me what that was at that time, possibly a partner.

Denny started walking over to the mine. I told him to put a hardhat on, and he looked at me like he knew what he was doing, kind of a sarcastic look. I turned around and asked Charles what he knew about the mine. He told me that he knew another man that had a claim next door to us and that he had known him for quite a number of years. He said we should get him to come over and show us how to mine this particular area as he had been doing it for years. I didn't like the sound of that. If I was going to run the mine, I didn't need somebody telling me how to do it, except for my boss. I told him that I had passed an older man on the road coming into the mine several times. He told me, "Yes, that's Doc."

I acknowledged him then turned and looked at my boss and said, "What do you want to do?"

He said, "Ask him if he would come over for a couple weeks."

"What do you want to pay him?" I asked.

He looked at me and said, "We'll talk about that later."

I said, "Well, we are gonna try to keep the cost down because you said if we didn't do that, we would have to go home and shut it down." I wasn't ready for something like that. I finally just said, "Okay. I'll talk to him." Then we walked over to the plant.

The miners had brought out several mine-car loads of ore and the amount that I had pushed up with the bulldozer was enough to start the plant up. We ran the ore that came out of the mine. Then we ran the pile that I piled up with a D8 cat. We shut down and went down to look in the sluice boxes.

Denny was standing over them all excited saying, "Man! Look at all of the gold in here!"

I looked in and told him, "This is mostly fine gold. It will take more gold than that to pay for the diesel to run the plant today. What you see here, hopefully we will see a lot more of. This is just a trial run. We will run for a week, then we will check it again. You can come up and get whatever we have and take it back down to Vallejo."

Denny said, "Okay, I'll be here Friday, and I will bring the paychecks."

"That'll work," I said and they got in their car and left the mine. They were going to Forest Hill for lunch and then going home. Actually, I was glad to see them leave.

The men came out of the mine tunnel, and I shut everything else down. I congratulated them on a good day. "Is there any other thing that you may need?"

They all said, "No."

"Are you guys happy with the job you are doing?" I asked.

"Yes," was the answer.

"Okay. We will start again in the morning. We will drill a round and shoot it then bring out the ore then drill another round for the next day."

They agreed to the plan. The men said goodbye and left.

I walked into the trailer, got a beer, fixed myself some dinner, and went to bed early. Another day was done.

CHAPTER SEVEN

The next morning, I sent Mike into the mine tunnel with John to drill the first round for the day. I took Randy with me in my truck and took off over to find Doc about a half a mile away from the mine. I came up to an old house. A man and a woman were standing outside in the yard. I drove up to him and told him who I was.

"Is your name Doc?"

"Yes," he answered then introduced his wife to me.

"Would you like to have a job for two or three weeks? Your friend Charles told me that you were a friend of his and that you knew a lot about the territory. I'll pay you $300 a week if you will come over and run the drill."

"Okay, I'll be glad to. Tony and Charles stopped by on their way out and told me to come over to see you."

"Can you start Friday?" I asked.

"Yes," he said. Doc was a small man, about 140 pounds with gray hair. His wife was a little heavyset and seemed to be a real sweet lady. She invited me to dinner that night.

I thanked her but said, "It will have to be some other time."

When I got back to the mine, Mike had come out of the mine and was working on something. "What are you working on?" I asked.

"The old drill isn't working right," he explained.

I asked Doc to come over and run the drill so that Mike could take care of the plant. "We will push up some more dirt outside to run through the plant at the same time we are running ore out of the mine."

He said, "Okay, but we'll have to do something about this drill."

"We'll give it to Doc and see what he can do," I advised.

"Okay," was all he said.

We went into the mine tunnel and loaded the holes and shot them. We would muck the mine out in the morning. Mucking is material removed in the process of excavating or mining. I told Randy that while Doc was there, I wanted him to stay outside and help Mike clean up around the plant when it was running. The day was over, so we shut down and went home.

I was bored with my trailer. I thought I would just drive up to the old store and see what was going on there. When I arrived at the store, there were some people that Moe knew standing there with a healthy German Shepherd. I made the comment that it was a beautiful dog.

"Do you want him?" they asked me.

"Who does he belong to?" I asked.

"He belonged to a highway patrolman," they explained. "But the dog didn't like loud noises so they were going to put him down. We took him, but we can't keep him. Can you take him?"

I looked at the dog and thought, *Well I might as well have a friend; it is kind of lonely in the mine.* So, I put him in the truck. He seemed to like the ride all the way back to the mine. I let him out when I got to the mine and we walked around for a while. He seemed to like me, I guess. He wasn't running away. He had big black patches around his eyes, like a mask, so I called him Bandit. I thought that would suit him fine. I fed him some hamburger I had, and he laid down in my trailer and spent the night with me.

I was impressed the next morning when the men came in and he growled and barked at them. I thought, *Good! A watch dog to let me know when the bad guys were coming in.*

Mike asked, "Where'd you get the dog?"

I said, "At the store."

He said, "That figures. Did they steal him?"

I said, "No. He's mine now."

Mike put his hand down to pet him, and Bandit licked his hand. Mike said, "I think he is a good dog."

I agreed then said, "Let's go to work."

We went into the mine to muck out the blast from the day before. We would pile it up outside for Friday morning. We would run it all through the plant before Denny got there with our paychecks. This way he could take whatever we found in the sluice boxes home with him. When he left to go home, things went well through the next the week. The drill was still giving us problems. I told Mike I would have the boss send us a new one.

Doc came over Friday morning. I introduced him to the men and had Mike take him into the mine and break him in on the drill. He said he had run a lot of drills and would not have a problem running this one. I suggested that we get started, so he went into the mine. I sent John in with him to watch his back. Mike ran the cat for the rest of the day, and I did some paperwork. I would check the fuel and take care of some other small things around the plant—cleaning out around the tail pulley and greasing all the spots on the plant.

Denny came in late. We had cleaned out the sluice boxes and put the ore in five-gallon buckets for him to take back. He was upset he didn't get to see what was in these sluice boxes before we put it in the buckets. I don't know what he was thinking, but if he was thinking we were taking any of it, he was dead wrong.

I told him, "If you want to have this ready to look at when you get here, you're going to have to get here earlier."

He didn't look too happy with me. He handed me the checks, loaded the four five-gallon buckets in his pickup and took off, but not before I told him to load the junk drill and bring another one up.

He said, "I'm not gonna load it. You leave it here and use it. I'll bring you another one Friday."

I told him, "Well, we won't get much done until Friday without a new drill."

As he left, I was thinking Doc and John have been in the mine twice as long to drill the nine holes as they should have been. I told Mike, "Let's go in and see what he's doing."

When we went in, the drill was running full blast. We shut it down. I asked Doc, "How long does it take you to drill four holes?"

"All day," was his reply. He said, "Boy, this rock is hard. So, we pulled the drill steel out, and I looked at the bit. It was completely worn down.

I told him, "Just stop, and we'll pack the drill out of the mine. Lay it on the ground by our work trailer." We would not use it anymore the rest of the week. We would run the rock from the outside that the D8 cat was pushing up until we received the new drill. I told Doc to go home, take the week off, and to come back next Monday. I used the rest of the men to clean up around the mine all week.

By Friday at noon, we had run all of the outside material the cat had pushed up. Now we were just letting the plant clean itself out, and we would wait for Denny to look into the sluice boxes.

When he arrived, it was around 4 o'clock, and he drove directly over to the sluice boxes. He stood 5′4″ and was a little stocky. He carefully put his pink gloves on and started tearing the plant apart, to see what was in the boxes.

"When you finish tearing up the place, you can put it back together!" I warned him. I'm sure I looked intimidating to him. He just looked at me, filled his buckets, and handed the paychecks to John. He unloaded a brand-new drill and jack leg out of his truck, got his buckets loaded, and left. He never said a word to me.

John handed me the checks, and I passed them out to each man and told them all to have a good weekend.

I decided I would drive out to my mom's house. I wanted to call Tony and ask him what the heck was going on. I got in my truck, loaded my dog, and took off for Auburn. Everything was locked up, and so far, I had no problems with anybody coming to my place. I would return Sunday night.

My mom was happy to see me and just happened to have some spaghetti and an apple pie ready for me. I got there just at the right time. Before dinner, though, I called my boss and told him what had transpired.

"Sometimes kids just have to be seasoned more," he explained.

I said, "Well, I don't want any problems with your son or anybody else."

He said, "I understand. Don't worry about it. I'll be up next weekend and will bring my wife up to see the mine, maybe do a little panning."

"That'll be great," I told him.

Tony said, "I'm going to bring a house trailer up there so we can stay overnight."

I assured him, "That'll be fine. We'll make a place for it." I would have to tell the guys to be on their best behavior if the boss was there.

"There was six and a half ounces in the last bucket," he informed me. "That is just barely enough to pay for our cost, but that's okay, as long as we can keep it there or above."

"We were running outside material because the drill that Denny originally brought up was no good," I explained.

He said, "Well, he was supposed to bring up a brand new one."

"He didn't. He brought up an old one. It was a junker. He did bring a new one up today."

He didn't say much after that. I wished him good night and told him I would see him the next Friday.

I had a good visit with my mom, and I left Sunday around 4:30 in the afternoon to go back into the mine. On the way out, I decided to go to Grass Valley to the Coach House. It was a bar and restaurant. They had a live band on the weekends. When I walked into the bar, I was surprised to see Mike and his wife, Diane, and his sister sitting at the table having a drink, so I went over and sat down with them. The man playing the music was a friend of mine. His name was Rocky. He was very talented. It felt good just to relax a little bit.

I told Mike, "Don't come to work with a hangover. I don't think Tony was too happy with what we are taking out, so you and I are going to look inside the mine tomorrow and make some decisions."

CHAPTER EIGHT

The underground river channel is the same as a regular river running on top of the ground. The gold usually is deposited on the inside turns of the river, and the bedrock had to be facing toward the way the water is running to catch the gold in the crevices. We would have to decide where we were in the river to be able to find both sides of it and to know which direction to head. The old timers would follow the little green rocks, as they were iron ore and heavy. Where you saw them, you would find color. So, we were going to look over the face of the mine the next day.

Monday morning was cold. Mike and I walked into the mine with a bright light to look over the face. It was obvious that the right-hand side of the river had a steep bank on it where I had looked down from the Chinese tunnel, so that was the right side. We would turn the tunnel to the left and go across and see if we could find the left side. Then we would know how wide the river was, and we would follow the little green rocks.

I set Doc up on the face with the new drill with John helping him, and we started the drill. It went fast. The drilling was done in less than an hour and a half. We were thinking we could even get two shots off that day. What a difference a new drill made! We loaded the holes and shot them. We would wait for the smoke to clear out. I sent everyone in to help muck it out and fill the mine cars so we could get another shot drilled before the end of the day. I wanted to work hard this week, to try to get a good pay for my boss. We would all work our tails off.

I noticed after a while that Doc was drilling above the bedrock with his lifters. The lifters are the last three bottom holes drilled for the dynamite. If you didn't get down into the bedrock, you wouldn't find the gold because it would always be lying on the bedrock or in the cracks of the bedrock, so we had to pull the track up and start again. This did not make me happy. That set us back a day. We had to pull the track up and start over in order to lower the tunnel.

The next morning, Mike and I went into the tunnel to drill. I put Doc, John, and Randy outside to cut timbers to go into the tunnel. I looked behind me, and there was Bandit, his ears laid back, lying down, watching me even with all that noise, I couldn't believe it, but that would be short-lived.

That night after everyone went home, we had a lightning storm. When I got up the next morning, Bandit was gone. I looked all over for him, then I had the crew look for him. I couldn't find him anywhere, so everyone else went to work. I took the truck and went up on the road to see if I could find him. I drove all the way to the Iowa Hill store. I stopped there to see if they had seen Bandit. I noticed the large front window was broken out of the bar and as I walked in, there was Bandit.

Moe said, "Sometime during the night when it was just a terrible lightning storm, your dog jumped through the front plate window to get out of it.

I said, "Oh my God, what will that window cost?"

He said, "I don't know, but I'll send you the bill!"

I looked Bandit over and didn't see any cuts or marks on him, I loaded him up in the front seat of my truck and left. I took him back to the mine and tied him up to the trailer. There was a chance of lightning the next two days, and I was not gonna pay for every window in Iowa Hill. Everybody thought that it was real funny, but me. For the rest of the week, every time we were gonna shoot dynamite, I would tie the dog up at the front entrance of the tunnel. It would sound like a canon every time a shot went off. I was hoping he would get used to it. I didn't know then, but over time it would work.

It was Friday morning, and everyone showed up at the mine. My boss didn't bring his travel trailer. Tony and his wife, his friend Charles, and Denny were there to clean up the sluice boxes and to collect the gold. We were ready. The plant had run all week, and I was hoping for a good pay-out for Tony to take home. I set up some washtubs, filled them with water and the tailings from the sluice boxes I had in five-gallon buckets.

I put several shovelfuls in each gold pan and handed them a gold pan each. Tony, Denny, and Tony's wife all started panning gold. To my amazement, they were finding quite a lot in their gold pans and grew excited, but after a while, their hands got really cold. I ended up putting everything in five-gallon buckets for them to take home. They had a processing machine at my boss's house in Vallejo.

They processed what we gave them down there to separate the gold from the dirt. I had no idea of what the finished product was or how much they got, and I really didn't want to know. I could tell by looking at the sluice boxes if it was good or not. The following week, Tony said he recovered about twelve ounces. That was a good run, but it was not that much for a whole week. My payroll was around $2400 a week including the diesel, so we had to make more than that in one week to be able to break even.

Spot gold in 1981 was $400 an ounce on the river. The miners only got three-quarters of spot for the gold that they would pan and sell down on the river, so we really had to work hard if we wanted to stay here for the long haul.

Everyone went home. That would give me a chance to walk into the mine by myself. I would look at the cemented gravel in the walls of the tunnel to see which way the water had run when this was a live running river maybe millions of years ago. I was taught how to do that by some of the old miners that I knew as a kid who worked underground river channels. I had worked in hard-rock mines, but that would not help me here. That was altogether a different type of mine that would take an altogether different approach. I would work off of what I had learned as a child growing up with miners who worked it for a living back then.

The old timers used a little tool called a Picky Poke. The best way to explain this tool is it was like a screwdriver with a sharpened curved point on the end.

They would use it to dig into the face of the wall in the tunnel to loosen up the rocks to see which direction they were lying and then look for nuggets. If the flat rocks were tipped up at an angle, that would tell them the way the water ran back when it was an active ancient river. If the flat rocks were tipped up and bent to the left, that would tell them that the river was making a turn to the left. The same would apply to the right in any river on the surface or underground. Usually, if it was carrying gold, the old miners would look for the inside turn. That was where the river would slow down and deposit the gold, either the left inside or the right inside turn, and that was what I was looking for. Crossing the river with the tunnel would give me a mental picture of the old river and the way I would go.

I walked out of the tunnel and over and sat down in my chair. Bandit was there with me. I was petting him and thinking, *How in the world did it come to this? I love mining, but I sure miss my kids.* I looked around and thought, *Well, maybe we will go for a ride.*

I put Bandit in the front seat and rolled the window down a little so he could stick his head out. Then we started up to the store. I thought it would be nice to talk to Moe for a while. About two miles up the road I saw a Volkswagen pulled over and two men standing outside. I pulled up behind them and asked them what the problem was. They said they had a front flat tire.

I walked over to look at it. As I passed the one man, he hit me with a pipe on the back of my head and my shoulder, and I went down like a rock. I started to get up, and he raised his arm to hit me again. About that time, Bandit tore into him. I don't know how the dog got out of that truck, but he did and that gave me time to get up and knock the other guy over the bank. He rolled down about 15 feet, and the fight was over.

I went back to my truck and got my shotgun out and pointed it at them. I told them to get the hell out of here before I filled their butt with buckshot. I told them I never wanted to see that car on the hill again. They took off. I don't think that tire was as flat as they said it was. They just heard me coming up the road and was going to rob me.

I went up to the store and told Moe what had happened. I told him to call the sheriff.

"I would," he said, "but the phone lines are down from the storm. The old man that takes care of it is sick."

"No phone?" I asked.

Moe said, "That's right; it only works once in a while."

I knew right then I would be packing guns for the rest of the time I would be there. He gave me some ice and a clean cloth to place on my head and shoulder. It hurt pretty bad, and I was hoping that they hadn't broken my collarbone. I went back to the mine. I spent the rest of the day with ice on my shoulder.

The next morning when the men came in, I could hardly move around. I told Mike what had happened and that he would have to drill today until my arm got well. He was worried about me.

I told him, "I think I'm gonna be okay. I just need to take the day off today."

Mike said, "I'll take care of everything. Why don't you just go down to your mom's for a couple days and take a break? Call your kids and get some rest. I'll stay here tonight and watch things until you get back."

"Thank you. I think I will do that." Bandit and I got in the truck and went to Auburn to my mom's. After some much-needed rest and several phone calls to the kids, I went back up to the mine on Wednesday morning. When I got there, everything looked great. Mike was cleaning out behind the plant.

I walked over and asked him, "How are things going?"

"I think we should let Doc go," was his reply.

"What's the problem?"

He said, "He was going inside the mine with a gold pan."

I said, "A little high grading maybe." I smiled then told him, "Well, I really didn't like the episode with the drilling, and he wasn't really doing that well. I'll tell him we are just going to have to cut back. You and I will have to do the drilling until we get a better cleanup."

He agreed. I walked over and told Doc that we were going to cut back, thanked him for what work he had done, paid him off, and let him go. He left on good terms. He was our neighbor, and that was important to me. I would tell Tony when I called him the next week.

CHAPTER NINE

The next two weeks, we just drove tunnel. I stayed at the mine. Mike would bring in groceries and also beer for the boys that would come back and forth from Iowa Hill.

Randy told me, "There's another guy that I met up at the store who wants a job. Do you want to talk to him?"

"Okay. Send him down," I instructed.

"I'll bring him down with me," Randy said.

"Well, how's he gonna get home?" I asked.

"I guess he'll just walk."

"Whatever," I said.

The next day we were working on the plant. We had broken one of the wheels that the plant turned on, and Mike was trying to weld it to get us back in operation. Two guys came into the mine in an old junker truck. It was Randy's friend that he had met up at the store, and another man was with him.

I asked them what their names were. One man was Russell. The other one was Danny. I told them that when I had time, I would talk to them and that they could just wait over by the trailer. Mike and I worked on the plant for about an hour, and he got it fixed, so I went back over to talk to the two guys.

I first asked Russell where he had come from and a little about his history. He told me that he was an ex con and that he did some time for stealing from an ice cream truck.

I started to chuckle and looked over at Danny and asked him where he came from. He said California, but he didn't have any bad history. He told me that he was just a ladies man.

"Well, there are no ladies in here right now, so if you want to work here, keep your ladies out of here." I offered them both $200 a week for 40 hours. That wasn't a whole lot but for what I was getting to hire off the bank, it was a lot more than they would get anywhere else on Iowa Hill.

I asked them where they were staying, and he said in the old camper that they had for their truck and that they would bring it down and stay in the mine. I said, "Fine, but if you steal from me, you will have hell to pay. Got it?" They said they understood, and I told him they could start the next day doing mostly cleanup work and a lot of shoveling.

I went out that afternoon and called Tony and told him that I had hired two men. I gave them their names and social security numbers so Tony could put them on the payroll.

Tony agreed to the hire but cautioned, "Let's keep it down though. We're just breaking even."

"I'll do the best I can," I assured him. "I'm thinking about going in a different direction."

"Whatever you wanna do is fine with me," he stated.

On the way back in, I stopped at the store and asked Moe if he knew the guys that I just hired.

"They have only been on the hill for a couple of days and were broke," he told me.

"Well, if they need something, put it on a tab and I will take it out of their paycheck until they get started," I said. He agreed to do that.

Kup was there with Little Kup. He came over and gave me a hug so strong I felt a rib crack. I knew it was all in fun, but now I had to put up with that pain. I left and went into the mine.

CHAPTER TEN

The next morning, I put Danny on the loader and showed him how to feed the plant. I put Russell and Randy on the task of cleaning up around the plant. Mike and I went into the tunnel to drill. John would cut some timbers that day. For the next three weeks, we all did the same job.

One morning after a shot, Mike had gone back in to see how it went. He came out and yelled for me to come in and look. I went into the mine and walked up to the face where we had drilled. We had broken into an old tunnel—a Chinese tunnel—that possibly came in from the other side of the ridge. I could see the bedrock going up so I knew that we were across the river. With the Chinese tunnel there, there would be no reason to go on any farther. We would back up and go the direction I wanted to go, the direction I told Tony about.

We pulled the drill and the pipe and hoses back to the right side of the mine again and started a new face going in on a 45° angle. The first two shots were a lot better, showing more gold. We were going into a right turn in the river. I was excited about that now. Maybe we were making good progress. We went in about 30 feet and mucked it out and ran that dirt through the plant. It was about 18 ounces. I was really excited. That would mean that we might start making a little pay above breaking even.

My boss brought me up a new truck, a four-wheel-drive Ford with a CB radio in it that I could use to call him in Vallejo. We had a secret word that I would give him if we had gold for him to come get. I would tell him, "The cat's got my tongue." That would give him or Denny a reason to come up and pick up the buckets.

It had been getting real cold lately with several days of rain, and that night it started snowing. I told the guys to stay home. Mike said he would come in anyway. I warned him about the dangerous roads. I told him we could drill and shoot, but we would have to wait to muck it out.

That night, it snowed more. Then it started raining. Water was washing mud back down into the tunnel. We would have to weld a door on the tunnel and dig it out in order to stop it. We worked all morning in the pouring rain to stop the mud from going into the tunnel. That would be a disaster for us to dig out. Then it turned to heavy snow.

Mike informed me he would have to stay in overnight. That was no problem, but I worried that his wife may not have been prepared for that. He explained that he told her he might have to stay.

He went over to his truck and brought back a bottle of whiskey. I was so cold I couldn't see a reason why I wouldn't have a drink of it. After several drinks and feeling like we were starving to death, we decided we should go to Forest Hill for dinner.

There was over a foot of snow on the ground at that time, and we had a bucket of cleanup that I knew had a lot of gold in it. I didn't know what to do with it.

Mike said, "I do." He went out and got a shovel full of mud and put it in the bucket on top of the gold and said, "Let's go to Forest Hill. Nobody will steal a bucket of mud."

We plowed snow with the four-wheel-drive to Forest Hill and had dinner and a few more drinks before deciding it was time to go back to the mine before we couldn't get there because the snow was really starting to pile up on the roads.

I went to my truck and realized I had left the keys in it. I took a hammer out of the back toolbox and broke the small wing window out so I could reach in and open the door. We started back. I would be lying if I didn't say we were really buzzed. We laughed all the way about what they would think when they went to clean up the bucket and found it had mud in it. We made it back to the mine and crawled into bed.

The next morning, Mike went back home. The road was open. I stayed in. There was no point in going out. I was really depressed, and I had a bad headache. Going to Forest Hill was a bad idea. The bottle of whiskey was a bad idea.

Bandit and I just walked around in the mud looking over the area. I was really feeling sorry for myself, so I went back to the trailer and finished off the rest of the bottle of whiskey.

After a time, I realized that I was cold and we were out of wood for the stove. I took the chainsaw outside. Up above my trailer was a little Madrone tree. I decided I would cut it down and have some wood for my stove. I wasn't in any condition to do any logging. My judgment was way off. When I cut the tree, it fell on my trailer and broke a window out. So now, not only did I not have any wood, but I also had a hole in my trailer with the wind and rain coming in. It was terrible. I woke up about midnight with a dog lying on top of me. I don't know if he was trying to keep me warm or if he was trying to keep warm.

I was miserable. I was in a real dark place. I thought that's probably where some people consider suicide, but that wasn't me. I vowed to stick it out. Thank God it started to get better.

After about three days, the sun was up when I got up in the morning. It was a beautiful day. I went outside with Bandit and went for a walk about 100 yards from the trailer. I saw his hair go up on his back, and he started growling. I looked around and didn't see anything—no bears or mountain lions. I happened to look up in a tree, and there was a cougar looking down at us. It was not a very big one, but big enough for me to get out of there. I grabbed Bandit by his collar and drug him back to camp, tied him up, got my gun, and went back, but the cougar was gone. I was thankful for that, I had no plans to shoot him, but I thought I would just scare him hoping he would leave.

About that time, I heard a siren. It sounded like it was coming from Iowa Hill. It was really loud and kept coming closer and closer. I started getting worried. I hoped something hadn't happened at home or to my mom. I thought, *Maybe it was Doc or his wife.* It got louder and louder, then it started coming down the ridge toward the mine. I stood out in the open when I got a glimpse and spotted Mike's truck. Randy was driving it and Mike had an old siren hanging out the window, hooked to a battery, laughing his head off.

The thought came to me to pound his ass. "You scared the hell out of me!" I shouted, then we all started laughing. It seemed to me to be the start of having some fun getting back to mining and taking my mind off all the junk that I had been thinking. Thank God for that.

I told Mike that we would clean up the plant and let it dry out for the rest of the week and said he could pick up the guys in Iowa Hill the next Monday, and we would get started again.

He agreed. We laughed some more about what he had done. It seemed to change my whole mood. Even Bandit was happy with me.

That Friday, Denny came in and brought some checks that the guys had coming. He picked up the bucket, looked in it, and said, "What's this."

I said, "That's your gold."

"What's with the mud?" he asked.

I said, "It rained."

He looked at me with disapproval.

I answered with, "Tell your dad and mom hello."

He just looked at me again, never said a word, and left. I put Bandit in the truck and headed up to the Iowa Hill store.

I knew the guys had a tab up there to pay, and they hadn't had a check for two weeks due to Denny not coming up because of the weather, so I wanted to get some money to them. When I got there, Randy was there with some other people—his mother, his sister, and her boyfriend.

Doc came over that afternoon and asked me if I would like to come to his house for dinner. He had asked me once before, but I never gave him an answer. I told him I would like that. Doc and I didn't have a problem. He wasn't mad at me for letting him go. He had plenty to do on his own claim.

I went over that evening and had a very nice evening with them and a very good dinner. I thanked them and went back home and went to bed.

I woke up about four in the morning thinking about what I would do Monday. I had cut some wood and put a cover over the hole in the window. I would build a fire in the little old stove and warm the place up and make a pot of coffee. I also made out my list of things that I would do Monday.

The previous few weeks had been cold. I was looking forward to spring, and it was coming. With that, I would be anxious to start the new tunnel farther back. The next few weeks were uneventful. We drilled shot and mucked out day after day. Denny would come up and get the buckets and bring the checks. Things were really going good, and I wasn't having any problems with the men.

Tony said we were breaking even, but I thought we were doing better than that. He would always tell me, "Well, you have to keep cutting back." But I was cut back to the bone. I just couldn't understand what Tony was talking about. I figured something was sketchy with the person picking up the several five-gallon buckets of gold.

Then one morning, Danny told me he was going to leave and live with some woman. He was constantly telling us guys that he was a ladies man, a lover. I was sick and tired of listening to his x-rated stories. I was glad to see him go; I gave him his checks and he left. Now we were down one, I would wait before I would tell Tony, to see if we still had to cut back more.

We were running out of 20-pound rail track in the mine; we needed to find more. We didn't know where we would go to get it. We looked around at some of the old mines to see if there was any lying on the ground but there wasn't any. Someone told Mike up at the bar that there was a lady that had a stack of rail track that she wanted to sell. They told Mike how to get to her place, so we took the mine truck (that was not licensed) to go get it.

When we got there, she was waiting for us. I thought, *Boy, word gets around up here fast.* "How much do you want for it?"

She said, "Five hundred."

"That's too much," I answered.

"Well, that's it."

I reached in my pocket and pulled out three one-hundred-dollar bills and a fifty-dollar bill. "That's all I got."

"I'll take it," she said without hesitation.

We loaded it up and took it back to the mine. It was in 12-foot sections; just right. The next week I had two more buckets for Tony. I called him on the radio and said, "The cat's got my tongue."

"Well, it is my birthday, and I'm not coming up there. Bring it down here."

I said, "Okay. I can do that." It would give me a chance to see the kids and get away from the mine.

I had my own truck in there, too, so when I got ready to leave, Mike asked, "Can I drive your new truck—your four-wheel-drive?"

I said, "Well, you better ask Tony." I called him on the radio and told him what Mike wanted to do. He gave his approval but told me to tell him to be careful.

I had a lump on my back that was giving me trouble, so I told Mike I was going to go by the doctor and have him look at it, and if he decided to cut it out, I would probably be gone for a few days. He would have to stay at the mine and keep running it until I got back. I trusted him and knew he would do a good job.

He said, "No problem. Get back when you get back."

I went down to Tony's house, gave him the buckets, and picked up some extra money to have around in case we needed to buy anything else. He was happy. It seemed like he was doing good. We must've been breaking even or doing better because he wasn't griping at me to cut things back. I told him that I laid off Danny and now had a shorter crew. I explained to him about my back and that I might not go into the mine for a few days.

He asked, "Is the mine still working?"

"Absolutely!" I assured him. "Your man Mike is running it." Then I smiled. I told him I would see him later.

"Okay. Be careful. Let me know how things work out on your back."

I told him I would. That week I wound up having surgery on my back for a benign tumor. I stayed at a friend's house. I would be all right going back to the mine in a couple of days.

Mike called me that night and told me he had wrecked my truck. I asked him what the hell happened. I wanted to know the truth. He had stopped at a bar on the way home and had a few drinks and accidentally backed into a car. He said he took off too fast and took out about 20 mailboxes on a turn.

The truck was in the shop and mailboxes were still falling out from under the truck. I told him that he would have to call the boss and tell him the news. I was sick. He said the cops had come to the scene of the mailboxes as they were hauling the truck away and gave him a ticket for driving too fast. Thank goodness they didn't know he had been drinking or he would've gone to jail. Now I would be driving my own truck or the old truck in the mine.

Denny went up with a flatbed truck and hauled the wrecked vehicle back down to Vallejo to the shop and said his dad was very unhappy.

I reminded him, "Well, he gave Mike permission to drive it. Now I will have to suffer because of it."

He said nothing.

Now I had no radio and never saw the truck again.

Denny would come in on every Friday from then on to check on us and get his bucket of goodies. When I got back to the mine, I noticed that the plant was shut down and nobody was around. I put away my groceries and walked down into the mine. They were working on the pipeline to the drill and filling some cars with dirt.

I asked Mike, "Why isn't the plant running?"

"We just ran out of dirt," he said.

"Why didn't you start the D8 up and push some up?"

He added in a sarcastic tone, "I can't do everything!"

I warned him, "Well, if you don't get this plant running, I'll get a new crew." I went back over to the trailer to take it easy.

After some time, he came over and apologized for wrecking my truck.

I reprimanded him. "From now on, if you want to drink, you do it on your own time. And that goes for everybody else smoking dope or whatever. This cost us, and we're not gonna be able to get things done screwing around!" He knew I meant it. I finished with, "Tomorrow, we will start like we did when we first were going full blast. We will drill two rounds tomorrow, and the plant will run all day."

I paid Russell off that night and laid him off. Now we were down to four: Mike, Randy, John, and myself. That is the way it would be from then on. We would carry the load.

It worked well for the next three weeks. Things were back to normal and we were doing pretty good. Nobody was complaining, not even Denny.

CHAPTER ELEVEN

One night, we were sitting around the fire. Everybody was going to stay in that night. They all had sleeping bags and tents.

Mike asked me, "How are things going with your ex?"

I told him, "I took my kids out to breakfast. My ex-wife got a hold of my daughter while we were in the restaurant on the phone and told my daughter to tell me that she hoped I choked on my food. Things aren't going very well as you can tell."

The next morning, I walked over to the mine entrance. Mike came out to meet me. He told me that about two hours before, a lot of water started running out of the ceiling. I told him we would go in and get the drill out of there and back up in the tunnel.

He asked me, "What are you thinking?"

"Water would not run out of the ceiling like that unless there is a sand pocket or a tunnel or a room above us. It's too dangerous to be in there until we figure out what's going on," I informed him.

Mike asked, "What's your plan?"

I replied, "We will timber it heavily up to that spot. We will take the drill and drill straight up just this side of where it's coming out to see if we break into something. If not, it's a sand pocket. We'll have to discontinue in that direction and go another way because there would be a danger of a cave in, and I'm not taking any chances."

He agreed with me, so we spent the rest of the day cutting 12-inch poles seven feet long to timber inside the tunnel around the area where water was running out of the ceiling. The next day after the timbers were in place, we set the drill up and drilled straight up in the tunnel ceiling for six feet and ran into nothing above us that would be open. I determined it must be a sand pocket, which was extremely dangerous. We backed out, pulled the drill back and the hose. We had to get ready to go another direction.

I decided we would talk about that after we got everything in place for a new direction. I had something in my mind that I had been looking at for some time. I had picked up a little five pennyweight nugget that I saw one morning going past this one area, and I thought we would have to check that out later, but now would be the time to back up and drill that direction.

That evening, as we sat around the bonfire, we had a discussion on safety in the mine and around the plant. I wanted everybody to take the next day off and we would go all through the whole mine inside and outside to see if there was anything that we could improve. Randy, John, Mike, and I would be doing this.

The next morning after we all got together, Mike asked, "Do you hear that horrible noise those birds have been making over in that brush? They've been screeching like that for the last two days and it's driving me crazy."

I said, "I don't know what kind of birds those are. Let's get to work and forget about the birds."

We spent the first four hours in the tunnel going through things in there, looking over loose rock or anything in there that might be a problem, checking our old timbers to make sure they were tight. Then we went outside for lunch. I went over to my trailer. John and Randy had their lunch outside. Mike disappeared after a short time.

I heard an explosion next to the mine. *What in the world was that?* I tore out of the trailer. John and Randy were laughing. I looked over at the brush. There was Mike.

They said Mike went to the powder magazine and got a stick of powder, put a cap in it, lit it, and threw it at the birds.

"You're kidding!" But I knew they weren't, so I went over to Mike. He was laughing, but I didn't think it was a bit funny. I chewed his butt out for half an hour. It was only after I calmed down a bit that I found it kind of funny.

Mike had always been a little crazy and, at this point, we had become very close. I really liked him. So, after a time, I laughed, too, and the birds were still squawking after we finished going over the plant and the outside equipment.

I told him they could go home, and I would pay them for the rest of the day. Randy told me that he had seen Russell up at the bar, and that he tried to borrow some money from him.

I said, "Well, I haven't seen him since it snowed and I laid him off. I guess he doesn't wanna make any money, and I wouldn't give him any money. I have a check here of his with about six hours work on it. You can take that up to him but tell him he'll have to find work somewhere else; he won't come back here.

After everyone left, I went in the trailer and got a towel and a bar of soap. I planned to go down the road and take a shower under the culvert pipe like I had done before. I got in the truck and went there. I could park where they couldn't see the truck or see me. I took my clothes off, got underneath the water, and was taking my shower when I heard a commotion up on the road.

I looked up, and there was a man on a motorcycle and a motorhome parked right behind him, and they were fighting over something. The man in the motorhome kicked him in the head and knocked him down. Then some woman came out of the motorhome with a rifle. I thought that there was going to be something bad happen very soon. I reached over and got my shotgun stepped out from under the culvert pipe and fired a shot in the air. The looks on their faces were priceless—a naked man with a shotgun. They both took off.

I heard later that they got into another fight up at the store, and the guy in the motorhome broke the jaw of the biker, and they had to take him out to the hospital.

With a short shower and a trip back to the mine, I was thinking *The nuts are running the asylum.* I went in the trailer and took a nap.

The next morning, Mike came in, laughing himself silly. He had stopped at the store to pick up some things for lunch. He said, "The people up at the store were talking about a crazy man, naked, running around with a shotgun. Is there anybody that you know that would do that?"

I said, "I don't have a clue; maybe Sasquatch."

He said, 'Yeah right," and we started laughing."

I told him the rest of the story and we had a good laugh. Then I said, "Now let's go to work."

He said, "Okay, if you say so. As long as you keep your clothes on." He smiled.

CHAPTER TWELVE

We started the new tunnel in an area that I could see had a lot of heavy iron rocks with a good sharp turn. We only went in six feet and ran that through the plant to see if there was anything in it. It lit up the sluice box. There was a lot of good pay in the first shot. I thought to myself, *Finally we've got into the area that I've been looking for.* We drilled another round and shot it. It took us till 8 o'clock that night to muck it out, but we were excited.

The next morning, I ran it in the plant, and it was the same. It had a lot of gold in it. I told Mike that from now on, he would have to stay in the mine with the men; not that I didn't trust them, but I wanted to make sure I wouldn't have something to blame them for. He said he understood. We agreed that John could work with him and Randy could work with me outside.

The next Friday, Tony came up by himself with the checks. I told him what we ran into and showed him.

"That's great!" he said.

I informed him, "I would like to raise Randy and John's pay from the $200 a week because now there's just four of us, and we're working hard. I think they're worth it."

He turned me down. I wasn't too happy about that. We had a few words but then everything calmed down.

He said, "I'll be up here next week, too. I'll be bringing my wife and will stay overnight."

"Okay. I'll make sure the batteries on your trailer are charged and hooked up to my generator."

He left with two buckets of high-grade. I was really proud of the men and how hard they worked. I told them that I would meet them up at the store and buy them all a beer and have a hamburger that evening.

When we all got there, there was a big commotion going on next to the building. I walked around to see what was happening. It was Russell and the guy that had the motorhome, and they were having a fight. The guy with the motorhome was about six foot two. Russell was just a little guy about 145 pounds and five foot seven, but he threw a good punch and knocked the big guy's front tooth out, so he reached over to a pile of firewood and grabbed a big stick to hit Russell in the head.

I jerked it out of his hand and told him if he was gonna fight like that, I would get in the middle of it, too, so they went back at it. Russell got a piece of his ear bit off, but after a while they quit. I think they were both wiped out.

When I was sure nobody was going to get killed, I went on in the bar with my guys from the mine and bought the beer and hamburgers. We played a little pool and had a good time for about two or three hours. Other people in there were now starting to accept the fact that we were going to be there for a while and decided not to mess with us.

Friday came. Tony and his wife came in. He told me that he got pulled over by the sheriff up by Colfax. They thought his car was involved in a robbery. It scared them pretty good before the sheriff realized that they were just two old people, and Tony explained to them where he was headed. It kind of shook him up and definitely shook his wife up.

She asked me, "What kind of place is this?"

I said, "A place you would not want to get stuck in without a gun."

Tony was quick to say, "I'll bring mine next time."

They put their things away and settled in for the night. That evening, they decided to take a walk out in the timber. They didn't go too far before running into a ton of landmines and toilet paper. Tony wasn't too happy.

I told him, "Well, we don't have running water and toilets in here, so the men kinda head out into the brush when nature calls.

He said, "I'll send you a toilet next week, and they will come in and pump it out every so often." Then he went back to his trailer being careful where he stepped.

The next morning, I took him in the mine and showed him where we were headed and explained to him what to look at. He was very pleased that we were headed in the right direction.

I told him, "This is mining. It's hot right now but, we might go two feet and find nothing, but right now things look good."

He said he understood and they would go back home that afternoon with some buckets. I don't remember them ever staying overnight in that trailer again all the time we were in the mine.

CHAPTER THIRTEEN

The next three weeks went good. There were times when I would go out to dinner or go down and see my mom to sleep in a clean bed and get a nice hot shower and a meal. I was happy with the way things were going, but that wouldn't last long. There was always something that would get your attention.

One night while the four of us were sitting around the fire, a big boulder rolled down the face of the cliff and missed the boss's trailer by about two feet. I thought maybe it broke loose on its own but then about that time, another big boulder rolled down within about three feet of us. I knew that something was going on above us.

I ran in the trailer and got my rifle. Mike grabbed his gun, and we ran out into the center of the flat, where our shop truck was parked. We could see up to the top of the ridge which was above us. We could see the top of a pickup truck and somebody up there.

I yelled, "If you roll one more rock down here, there's going to be hell to pay!"

A voice came back. "Is that so?"

With that reply, I put about eight rounds in a tree above the pickup truck from my M1 Grand rifle. Mike fired a couple shots into the cliff face, then we took off running for Mike's truck. We took off, with the wheels spinning, up the ridge. By the time we got to the top, all we could see were tail lights. I thought about shooting them out, but then common sense came to me not to do that.

I was on a hot mission to find out who that was, one way or the other. We went back down to the mine. Randy and John were really shaken up. I asked them if they had any idea who that would have been, but they said they didn't.

"Maybe you need to talk to Kup," Mike said. "I better stay in here tonight in case something else happens."

Randy and John would stay, too. I didn't sleep much that night wondering who would roll boulders down to try to kill somebody. *I'll make a trip into Kup's camp tomorrow to see if he has any idea who that might have been.*

Mike crawled out of his truck the next morning. He looked like he hadn't had a bath in two weeks. His hair was all messed up. I asked him if he was doing okay.

He said, "Yeah. I'm going with you today to Kup's camp. By the way, do you know any of the history of this place?

I said, "Yes, a little."

"Tell me about it."

I looked over at him and said, "Come sit down in the chair. I'll get you some coffee, and we'll talk about it."

The coffee was about two days old, but it would be good for him. I thought it was good enough for me that morning. I sat down and looked at him. "Mike, placer mining began along the American River and its tributaries soon after the beginning of the gold rush. Hydraulic and drift mining apparently began here in 1853 after the discovery of gold in 1848 at Sutter's Mill, and the onset of the gold rush in 1853. Miners prospecting the North Fork of the American River discovered gold along the north flank of the ridge between the North Fork of the American River and Indian Canyon. The miners made camp atop the ridge and christened it Iowa Hill, and from then on, the ridge became known as the Iowa Hill Divide. Further prospecting revealed that the rich tertiary gravel deposits were perched above the American River on the flanks and underlying the divide. After cessation of hydraulic mining, drift mining became popular again and continued through the 1900s. Tunnel mining prevailed."

He asked, "What's the history on the old town?"

"In 1857, the town of Iowa Hill was leveled by fire, never rebuilt to its prior state. The town burned down twice more in later years. So, there's not much left, just a few houses and that old bar. Let's get ready. I want to take a run over to Kup's. Leave your gun in your truck. I'll introduce you to him so he knows who you are."

He said, "I'll be ready in five minutes."

I told Randy and John to clean up around the plant, especially around the tail pulleys. Some gravel had fallen down and was jammed in there, and it needed to be cleaned out.

"We'll be back in about two hours," I told them. They went to work.

CHAPTER FOURTEEN

Mike and I drove on up to the hill and down on the little winding road that went into Kup's camp. We got about a half a mile in when we approached the first camp. Kup was there with one of the men I had met the last time I was over there and his family. I thought that would be perfect with none of the rest of them around, so we got out.

I introduced him to Mike and told him that he was my foreman and would be the one in charge when I wasn't around. He laughed and said that he was okay with that.

I told him what had happened at the mine and asked him if he knew anyone that would roll boulders off the ridge toward us.

"It wasn't anybody here," he assured me.

"I'm sure it wasn't you," I said. "I just wanted to know if you had any ideas."

"There's a group of druggies that live in a canyon about halfway between here and your place," he added.

I got out my map and had him show me where he was talking about. I couldn't believe it. It was on the creek that I had been taking my showers. "Go up the creek, past the General Grant Mine, and you'll find this old cabin on the left," he instructed.

"Whose old cabin?" I asked.

"Dirty Bob's cabin. I don't know how many are in there; they don't come around me."

I asked, "Do they have a pickup truck?"

He said, "I don't think so, but I don't know. Maybe."

"We'll check it out."

We left there and drove up to the store. I went in and asked Moe if he knew anything about the people that were living there. He said he didn't know anything about them, but the sheriff had come in with a helicopter and dragged some people out of there last year.

We left and went back to the mine. Randy and John had done a very good job cleaning up the plant, so I had them come over to the trailer. We opened up a beer and just sat around.

Mike asked, "How many mines are around us?"

I told him, "There's a lot of them. There is the Big Dipper, the General Grant, the Morning Star, the Gleason, just to name a few. We have to be careful not to trespass on those mines and that's underground, too. They all belong to somebody, but I don't see any reason why we can't go up that creek. We'll take the day off tomorrow, and then we'll work next Saturday to make up for it."

I finished the day, playing with Bandit and cutting some wood for the stove wondering what I would see by the creek.

The next morning, Mike didn't get in until nine. He had a flat tire on his old truck coming in. We got started up to the creek around 10. Both of us had strapped on guns, and I took my shotgun. We didn't know what we were gonna find. We would pass the General Grant up the creek about a half a mile and alongside of the creek was a big steam boiler that must've been used for a mine, so Mike and I looked it over.

I guess they heard us talking because we didn't go very far up the creek when I noticed two people standing up on the bank looking down on us, so we walked up to them. The man looked a little like Charlie Manson. He was skinny as a rail. I was thinking he could go through a crack of a door without even opening it. Alongside of him stood a dirty looking blonde woman. I will put emphasis on the dirty. She had a real good shiner and had some bruises on her arms.

"Did your woman fall down?" I asked him. "She looks banged up a little?"

"Nah, she just likes it rough," he answered.

I looked at Mike, and he looked at me like, *What is this?*

I asked, "Are you Bob?"

"Yeah," he said.

"Do you people in here have a pickup truck?"

He said, "No, man. We ain't got no truck."

His girlfriend was looking Mike over. She said something like, "You're cute."

Mike turned around and said, "I'm out of here."

They both looked stoned out of their minds. We told them goodbye and walked back down the creek to the truck. We still didn't know who had the pickup. I didn't want to think about it and figured that God was stopping me from figuring it out saving me from doing something I would regret.

When we got back to mine. I looked all over and couldn't find Bandit. Mike and I started calling him. I finally heard him bark. He was clear up on the 200-foot face looking down at us! About that time, he started down the bank. It is almost vertical. He started coming at an angle when he lost his footing and started rolling end over end until he got down to the bottom near the entrance to the tunnel. It was looking tragic. I figured he was dead.

We walked over there, and he was lying in the mud whining. I picked him up and took him back to the trailer. I got out an old sleeping bag and laid him on it. I could tell by looking in his fur that he was black and blue on one side, but it didn't seem that he had any broken bones. I would just have to wait and see how he would make it through the night. I guess he followed us that morning. I should've tied him up. I was sick about it. I was just getting to love Bandit.

The next morning when I got up, he was walking around and looked like he was going to be all right.

CHAPTER FIFTEEN

The crew all came in and we fired up the plant and started mining.

The next three weeks went by uneventful. The only thing we did beside mine was go out and get groceries a couple of times.

We were having problems with mud in our pond. I went out and called Tony and told him we would have to get a dragline to clean the pond out. He said he had an old one in the yard and would send it up. I told him Mike knew how to run a dragline. We had been mining for several months now and were keeping our head above water as far as breaking even on the cost to run the mine and "a little over" according to the boss. Mike and I now were doing all the drilling. We would take turns—he would do it one day, and I would do it the next.

One day while he was drilling, he came out of the mine as white as a ghost. He came over to me and said, "I'm not going in that mine by myself ever again."

"What's the problem?" I asked.

He explained, "While I was drilling, somebody touched me—laid their hand on my shoulder. When I turned around there was nobody there."

His hair was still standing up on the back of his neck. I started to laugh but then I decided I better not. He looked serious about what he was saying.

I assured him I would go ahead and finish it.

I walked into the mine and up to the face where we were drilling. The drill steel was still in the hole and the jackhammer was standing up. All I had to do was turn it on.

When you're drilling in solid rock, the water going through the drill bit creates a fog in the mine, and everything seems to close in on you except the light from your hardhat shining on the hole where you're drilling. It is a little spooky when you're doing it by yourself and the tunnel is all fogged in.

I finished the holes and put the drill back, went out and went down to the powder magazine and got the explosive to put in the holes. John and I went in and loaded the holes. We cut the fuses and were getting ready to light them. As I lit them, some water dripped out of the ceiling and landed on my lighter and put it out. The fuses that I had already lit were burning into the holes. I kept trying to light it.

About that time, John jerked it out of my hand and spun the igniter, like a fast draw gunfighter from the old west. It lit. I finished lighting the last three holes. We took off running down the tunnel. As we made the turn to go out through the entrance, the first hole went off and the wind from the blast blew my hardhat clear out of the tunnel. Mike thought we blew ourselves up, but we walked out with our ears ringing. That was a close one.

Mike said, "I think that damn mine is haunted!"

I told him, "No, it's not haunted. We'll drill again tomorrow. I'll do it if you don't want to."

He paused then said, "No, I'll come in with you."

I told Mike, "When you head out tonight, call Tony. We need detonating cord. It will work better for lighting the fuses." He assured me he would.

You can tie the detonating cord around the cut on the fuse and then go to the next fuse and the next and the next, then light the cord. It will light all the fuses for you while you're walking out of the tunnel. For safety, that would be a good move; no more lighting them individually.

The next day around 10 o'clock in the morning, I heard a truck coming down the hill and I thought, *I wonder if that's the pickup I'm looking for?* It came into the mine, that old brown truck. I knew it at first glance. It wasn't the one I was looking for, and in the truck was Kup, little Kup, Tom Tom, and Pappy Kup and a couple of their girlfriends. It was the first time they ever came into the mine.

Kup got out of the truck and said, "Don't shoot." He started laughing. "I brought you a present because of our friendship."

He had an old pillowcase in his hand with something in it. He handed it to me and I looked in. There was a hind quarter of a deer. It stunk to high heaven.

He said, "You better eat it soon or it will be spoiled."

I thought, *Are you kidding me? If I ate this, no telling what kind of disease I would come down with.*

In the next breath, he asked, "Can I borrow fifty bucks? I'll pay you back."

I thought for a minute and said, "Okay. I'll loan you the fifty dollars, but if I don't get paid back, you'll never get anything else from me ever again."

"Fair enough!" he agreed.

I said, "I think you guys better go now."

He said, "Okay, we're leaving. Can we come back someday?"

"Maybe," I said, and they left.

Mike came over and asked, "What was that all about?"

I said, "They brought dinner for tonight," and I handed him the sack.

He looked in the pillowcase, made a terrible face and about gagged. He took the sack, winding it over his head a few times, and slung it. It looked like it sailed for a mile. Then he came back and asked me, "Would you eat that?"

"Heck no! I thought you might like it though." I laughed.

He said, "Bullshit! I'd have to be pretty freaking hungry to eat that thing."

I loved Mike. He was a real mountain man. He would fight a buzz saw—not afraid of anything . . . but ghosts.

CHAPTER SIXTEEN

We had been driving three tunnels since coming into the mine. One of them was into the sand pocket that was discontinued, one that went into an old Chinese tunnel that was discontinued, and now the new tunnel following the little green rocks— epidote. Remember, they're heavy, and gold follows them. I was hoping for a good pay. When I checked the boxes that afternoon, they were full of good color.

I told Mike, "We need to call Tony and have him come up. Tell him, 'The cat's got your tongue.' "

Mike had been doing my phone calling going back and forth to his home every night from Grass Valley, and that was helping me out a lot but not giving me much time to get out of the mine for things that I would like to do, like see my kids or spend the night at my mom's. I was starting to get depressed again.

It was a Friday, and we were finishing up for the day. I heard a helicopter coming. It came in and sat down about 150 feet from the mine, blue dust flying everywhere. Out of the helicopter stepped my boss and the man that owned the helicopter. He was a contractor that had huge dredges that would work in the delta. His name was Billy.

I took them over to where we were doing the last cleanup. He was very impressed with my boss's mine. My boss was happy with where we were going at the time and the gold that we were finding. He handed me the checks for the week, loaded the buckets on the helicopter and they flew out.

We finished up for the day, and everyone went home but me. This was my home. It had been my home for over a year now. I was getting pretty sick of it. Looking at nothing but dirt and a heavy-duty machinery plant. The dust from the machinery covered the vegetation for quite a distance, so everything was basically one color.

Tony told me that his friend Charles had opened a mine down on the river, the old mine that was called the Truro. He said he wanted me to go down there and look it over and see what I thought about it. I thought, *Well, maybe that'll give me something to do to take my mind off of all the other things that are going on in my head.*

I had a rough idea on how to get there. I would have to go up to the hill and turn right and go past Roach Hill for about a mile and then turn down to the left on a narrow road that would go into the canyon and the American River. So, Saturday morning I took off to go there. I found the road going down in there and came to a gate. I thought, *Well, that's as far as I can go.* But, when I looked at the gate, it was unlocked. I was a little apprehensive about opening the gate and going any farther. *What the heck?* I thought. *They can't eat me. I might as well go.*

It was quite a distance down into the canyon. When the road stopped, there was a trail that went down to the river. There was a tunnel portal where I parked my truck. I saw a little cabin, so I thought I would walk down and see who was there. When I got close, a man stepped out of the cabin.

He said, "Hi, I'm Frank." Then another man came out. He introduced himself as Benny.

They were probably in their late 60s. I told them who I was and what I was looking for. They told me to come over and sit down and have some root beer.

Benny added, "I make good root beer."

I accepted the offer and started looking around. "How long have you guys been down here?" I asked.

Benny said, "A long time. This is our claim."

"I thought this was the Truro mine," I said.

Frank said, "It is, but our claim is down on the river. Some new people just took over the big claim."

I said, "Yes, I hear that it's a man named Charles."

Benny added, "Yes, he's going to start bringing equipment in here. I don't know if we're gonna like that at all. It's very peaceful here and quiet."

I asked, "Is there anybody else down here?"

Benny replied, "There's a woman that lives down on the river at the Tiltin' Hilton."

I about choked on my root beer, "The Tiltin' Hilton? What's that?"

"It's an old cabin that leans over the hill toward the river. She's been there a long time."

I thought to myself, *That's crazy. But from what I've seen up here, I'm not surprised.*

I spent quite a bit of time down there with those two old men. I really liked them. They showed me some of the nuggets they were getting out of the river and a nice dredge they had sitting in the river. I was impressed with them.

I said, "I don't see a vehicle. How do you guys get in and out of here?

Frank said, "We walk down the trail from the store."

"And that's the way you haul things in here?"

"Yes, that's what we do."

"How far is that, Benny?" I asked.

He said, "I don't know. Five miles maybe, straight up and straight down."

As I started to leave, I saw an old mine car that was lying there in good condition. "Does that belong to the big mine?" I asked.

"No, that's ours," said Frank.

I took a chance. "Do you want to sell it?"

They looked at each other and Frank said, "Well, we could. What would you give?"

"Name the price!"

Benny threw a number at me. "Three hundred."

I said, "If you help me load it in the back of my truck, I will give you three one-hundred-dollar bills."

In less than twenty minutes, I had it loaded and was on my way out of there, headed back to the mine.

When I got to the top of the hill, I pulled over and thought for a minute. *What did I just witness? Benny making root beer? Frank was sitting there looking at a bunch of old newspapers, out-of-date, talking about the condition of the country. Two brothers mining to make a living.* I felt like I just went back in the past to 1849. *Wow, that's the way it was back then—the old cabins, the gold pans, pics, and shovels.*

I thought about it for a while and actually got tears in my eyes. I knew for sure I would be going back to visit them again. I had a special feeling for those old men and I wanted to get to know them more. It really humbled me about what they did back then and what we are doing now.

I changed my mind about going over to the mine. Instead, I went past the store down the canyon across the bridge to Colfax and down to Auburn to my mom's house. I would leave the mine car there.

I spent the rest of the day and night there and Sunday. That afternoon, I went back into the mine. I sat down in my chair and got very emotional. I thought about God, my kids, and the way my life was going, and I just broke down and started crying. *What did I do wrong? How was this gonna end?*

I think it all started when I visited those old men and thought about what it was like in the old days. I thought about my grandfather, who had five children and had to edge out a living working in the mines, and how he would come home, lie down in front of the stove and bleed out of his mouth with miners' consumption, which would eventually kill him. I thought of my grandmother, who had a kitchen table that she had to leave because when they left when that mine closed down, they could only take what they could pack to the next mine, and how she told my mom she cried.

Something was going on in my soul. I would have to get myself together before Monday morning. I took the dog, and we went on a long walk. When I came back, I ate a little something, and I went to bed still with tears in my eyes. I dreamed that night that I saw God between two dry riverbeds, standing there looking at me. There were no trees, no brush, just dried up riverbeds. He didn't say anything, just stood there. I guess he was telling me He was there.

The next morning after about three cups of coffee, I wondered about the dream and what that all meant for me.

CHAPTER SEVENTEEN

I was glad to see Mike come in and, right after him, the rest of the crew. We would go to work that week and it went by uneventful except for one day. When we were working in the mine drilling, Randy said, "I just saw Denny walk down one of the old tunnels."

"Really?" was all I could say.

We shut the drill off. I said, "He must've come up early. I don't have a clue why he's walking down that old tunnel." I went over to the old tunnel and walked down to the end of it. No Denny, so I went back to the drill. I told Randy, "I didn't see him."

He said, "Well, he's here."

I said, "We're gonna finish drilling, and then I'll go talk to him." We were just finishing the last hole.

Randy said, "Well, now he's in the other tunnel looking. I just saw him go down there."

I said, "Okay." We shut down.

I went over to the other old tunnel, walked all the way down. No Denny. I went back and asked Randy, "Are you smoking dope again?"

He said, "I saw him, I saw him!"

I said, "Okay, I'll go out. He must be outside." We all went out there and there was nobody.

Mike said, "I told you the place was haunted."

I looked at him and said, "What do you mean by that?"

"Do you remember me telling you someone was touching me when I was drilling?"

I looked over at Randy, and he was pale.

I said, "There are some beliefs in the old mines of trolls and Tommyknockers. The old miners would hear noises underground pounding and popping. They thought that they were little people or ghosts of old miners. In any mine you hear that stuff. It's just the ground moving and as far as seeing people underground, I don't know what to tell you."

Randy said, "You don't believe me, do you?"

I looked at him and told him, "Really there's a lot of things that go on in this world that I don't know about, but I will tell you, if you saw it, I believe you. I also think that there's no threat to any of us in this mine as long as we believe in safety first. Mike, go get the powder so we can shoot the shot. If you don't wanna go in, John and I'll do it."

Mike got a little puffed up and said, "I don't have a problem going in there."

"Okay, Mike. Just forget it and get the job done today." The last thing that I was going to tell them was that it happened to me one day when I was drilling—somebody laid a hand on my shoulder in a firm grip. There was a lot of other things that I witnessed in mines in my lifetime, things that I saw that I couldn't explain. If you thought about that all the time, you would never go underground.

I told Randy that he was doing a good job at the mine. I didn't want him to think that he wasn't. I didn't want him going anywhere, and if it bothered him, he could stay outside and work around the plant. That was important, too. He said he was okay and was glad "we had this little talk." The rest of the day went by with no more problems. But I could tell by their demeanor that they were still thinking about it the rest of the day.

That evening, John and Randy went up to the store to have a hamburger. Mike and I sat down and talked about the day.

"How are things at home?" I asked him.

"Okay," he said.

I knew there was more to that one-word answer. "You're not spending too much time over here, are you?"

He said, "It's my job."

I said, "Yes, I know that, but you need to spend time with your wife, too. You've been spending some weekends here with me."

He said, "She sells real estate and is gone most of the time on weekends anyway, and she doesn't have a problem with me over here. But, I would like to take some time off for Thanksgiving. It's coming up in about a week."

"That's no problem. I would like to spend some time with my mom. My ex-wife will be in Auburn with the kids because her parents live there, too. That would give me a chance to be able to spend some time with them. I'd like to do something special for Randy and John. They don't have any family or any place to go. I think I'm gonna let them stay here in my trailer and bring them in a cooked turkey and some things to go with it. They sleep in their tent anyway. At least they'll have pots and pans and utensils. I think it would be a good idea. Besides, there will be somebody here to watch the place."

Mike agreed. "Yeah, that sounds like a good idea."

I told him I would go out Friday after the checks came in and get the stuff and bring it back in Saturday morning for Thanksgiving. Then I would go back out, so we worked the rest of the week.

Denny came in with the checks Friday and got the cleanup and left. I told John and Randy about what I discussed with Mike and they were excited. I left right after that and went out and would bring everything back in the morning. I stopped by the store on the way home and got a little turkey and some other things. When I got to my mom's house, I told her what I wanted to do. She put the turkey in the stove for me and said it would all be ready for me to take in tomorrow morning then asked me if I was coming back. I assured her I was and that I wanted to spend the next two days with her and be able to see the kids as well.

The next morning going into Iowa Hill, I felt really good about what I was doing for the guys. When I got down to the mine, they were there sitting in the chairs around the fire pit. I think they were just waiting for me. I told them to go ahead and use my trailer and to eat lots of goodies. I would see them Monday morning. They thanked me for everything. Then I left and headed back to Auburn to spend the rest of Saturday and Sunday with my mom.

We had worked clear through the week. Now we were enjoying Thanksgiving on the weekend. Mom was making some goodies in the kitchen, and I was just enjoying sitting back in the chair, knowing I didn't have to go back to work until Monday.

We had a wonderful dinner and were sitting around the TV in the evening watching Lawrence Welk, my mom's favorite show. Her friend Harry was there. He had been on the ranch for a number of years helping her so you might say he was a live-in boyfriend. I was looking forward to having the rest of the weekend off and seeing the kids on Sunday.

The telephone rang, and my mom went out into the kitchen to answer it. Then she called me to come. I said, "Who could it possibly be at this time of night?" I picked up the phone and it was Mike on the other end. He was screaming in my ear. I said,

"You going to have to calm down so I can understand what you're talking about."

He repeated himself a little slower and told me, "Our shop truck, the one that's not licensed, is sitting in front of a bar in Colfax."

I couldn't believe what he just said, and I made him say it again.

He said, "The truck is in the front of a bar. It has no license plate. I'm headed there now from Grass Valley."

I said, "Mike, listen to me. Don't go in there until I get there. Wait for me out front. I will be there as soon as I can get there." It would be at least a twenty-minute run from Auburn. I told my mom what had happened and where I was going. I told her not to worry and didn't know what time I would be back, but I knew I would not be able to see the kids on Sunday or stay there. I told her I had to take care of a problem. She followed me out to the truck and told me she was really worried that something might happen to me. I assured her I would be back when I could but maybe not until the next weekend, then I left.

When I got there, Mike was walking around his truck with a pick handle in his hand. I told him, "Put that away. Let's go see what's going on. Calm down."

We started in the door. Mike flung it open, hit a chair, and made a big noise. He walked in like he owned the place, and I was right behind him. It only took him a few seconds to spot John sitting on a barstool. He went over to him and grabbed him by the shirt, spun him around, and then had his hand on his neck. I grabbed him and pulled him off. John looked terrified. Mike, with his face about two feet from him, was letting out some profanities.

About that time, some woman on the other side of the bar threw a beer bottle at her husband. It flew across the room and missed Mike's nose by about three inches. He didn't even flinch, still screaming at John. I finally grabbed both of them and drug them out of there. When we got outside, I asked John where Randy was. He said he was down at his mom's house. I told Mike to go get him, and I would wait here with John and the truck until he got back.

He was gone for about twenty minutes, and then he came back with Randy. Now I had both of them together.

"What the hell were you thinking about driving the truck clear up here with no license on it and no insurance and leaving the mine?"

Randy said, "You wouldn't believe us even if we told you."

"Go ahead and try," I said.

Mike started yelling again. "Back off," I told him. "Let's listen to what they have to say."

Randy said, "We were having dinner in your trailer and everything was wonderful. Then John looked up and saw a big eyeball looking in the window. It was Bigfoot. I know it was. It scared the hell out of us. When it left, we took off and the truck was the only thing we had that we could drive that had keys in it."

Now Mike was really going crazy. "Bigfoot? Sasquatch? Really? What kind of weed have you been smoking? You're both fired! You'll never work at that mine again."

I turned around and looked at Mike. "I run the show up here, and I don't have time to look for two more dudes. Unless you want to do the work for three people, calm down. You take the truck and take it back to the mine. I'll follow you and then bring you back to your truck. He looked at me disgusted. I said, "Mike, please do what I'm saying."

He said, "Okay, I'll do it for you, but I am not through with them."

"I'll take care of it," I assured him.

Randy said, "I was so scared. I'll never stay in that mine again at night. I don't wanna lose my job, but I'm telling you the truth. It was Bigfoot!"

I said, "Okay, Randy. You get somebody to bring you and John to work Monday. If you don't show up Monday, you won't get a paycheck next Friday. You'll have to get somebody to bring you back and forth every workday."

Randy said, "Okay, we'll do that."

When Mike came back, I followed him into the mine with the truck. It was about midnight before I got him to calm down and got him back to his truck. I slept in Sunday morning. Bandit and I went outside and looked around. I saw the hair standing up on his back, and he was growling. I went back into the trailer and got my shotgun, and we walked over toward the portal of the mine. He kept growling, so I got a light and we went in the mine. We went through all of the tunnels and back outside and walked all over around the mine. I didn't see any Bigfoot tracks anywhere. I thought to myself, *I need to forget it.*

I cleaned up the mess that they left and threw out the rest of the food that had dried up. I sat down and opened a beer. This place was turning into a nuthouse. I finished that beer and opened another one when I heard a truck coming down the hill. I thought, *Oh my goodness, now what?* When it came into the mine, it was King Kup, Little Kup, Pappy Kup, and a couple of girls that I had never seen before.

He said, "I came over to invite you to come to our camp for Thanksgiving."

I thought to myself, *Are you kidding? After what I've just been through, and now I to have an invitation to go to Kup's camp.* I thought for a minute and I said to myself, *Why not?* "I'll follow you over," I told him.

About that time, I heard somebody yell behind me. One of the girls had walked over to our pond, slipped and landed in the mud, covered from head to toe. So, we took the hose from the mine, and Pappy Kup washed her off from head to toe. I couldn't help laughing at these characters.

 I took off and headed across the ridge to Kup's camp. When I got there, Fred and his family from the camp just above Kup's house was there, too, and a lot of other characters I'd never seen before. We sat down and ate something. I had no idea what it was, but it wasn't too bad. I knew it wasn't deer meat.

The party went into the evening and it was getting dark. They had a bonfire going, and everybody was sitting around it with whiskey, beer, and drugs. It was about 9 o'clock when Fred's teenage daughter told me she could shoot a bottle cap off with a pistol 40 feet away.

I told her, "You're nuts. I'll bet you twenty dollars you can't do that."

She said, "Give me your gun. I'll show you." She took aim and pulled the trigger and blew the bottle cap right off the bottle. I lost my twenty dollars, and everybody stood around laughing.

Kup asked me that night, "Does anybody call you by anything besides Jim? Do you have a nickname?"

"Yes," I said. "My uncle had a nickname for me. It was Bow Hawk. That's a nickname that I've had ever since I was five years old. I loved my uncle and he loved me. He loved to call people by comic book characters back then, and that was mine.

Kup put his arm on my shoulder and said, "From now on, we're going to call you Hawk Kup. You're going to be a member of my family.

I thought to myself, *Why not? These people are no threat to me or the mine. At least I'll have somebody to visit and maybe help some of them to get out of the lifestyle they're living.* So, I said, "Okay, but don't ask me to do something illegal. I won't have any part of that. Like you said, what you do is your business and what I do is my business. I'll be glad to be friends with you. I feel a lot better making friends than enemies on this hill." We shook hands, and Kup promised me that he would let me know if any bad people were on the hill to look out for and that he would watch my back if anything happened. I told him I appreciated that, and I would do the same for him.

CHAPTER EIGHTEEN

Things got back to normal the next week. We were driving tunnel and running the plant. Randy's mother was bringing John and him into the mine every day and picking them up after work. Mike told me one day that Tony had called him and wanted me to call him that evening.

I went up to the store, and the phone was working. Old man Swab had worked on the lines, so I called Tony. He told me that Charles was coming up and that he wanted me to go down into the Truro and see if I could give them some help with where to run the tunnel. I agreed to the task. I didn't have a clue about that, but I would go down and spend a day looking it over. At least I'd get to see Benny and Frank. I would take them down some goodies and spend a little time with them, too. I liked those old men.

The next morning, I drove down into the mine. I went down and saw Benny and Frank for a while. Charles was there, too. He had some men with him. He had brought in an old dump truck and some other equipment, and he wanted me to look at the tunnel. I told him I would, I went to the truck and got my light and started walking in that tunnel. In just a short distance, I could see huge boulders in the ceiling. It was dangerous ground. Some of those boulders had fallen down into the tunnel. I couldn't see a way that he could drive tunnel in that and be safe. Timbers just wouldn't hold it.

I said, "You probably will have to drive a brand-new tunnel. We would have to figure out where you would go in to get into the old works ahead of all these boulders." I went outside. I spent about two hours walking around, and then I found an old shaft that had to go down into the tunnel. It was an air shaft, a way for them to get in and out if the tunnel caved in. It probably had been used years ago when the mine was running. I spent the rest of the day with an eye level and 100-foot tape to figure out where I would drive a tunnel, if it was me, trying to get into the ground ahead of those boulders and the several cave ins.

At the end, I marked it with a big stake with ribbons on it and told him, "This is the direction I would go if it was me. You will have to make your own decisions."

I left and drove up the hill. I ran into a guy walking. He looked like a soldier with camouflage on. I stopped and talked to him for a little while. He told me he hated people and he stayed down there in the Truro to be away from people. He stated that he had a bad problem in Vietnam and had lost his whole platoon to friendly fire.

I asked him, "What do you do down here?"

He said, "I just stay away from people."

I asked Frank about him later. Frank told me, "All he does is catch rattlesnakes, cut the tails off of them and throw them in a hole somewhere that only he knows about."

I thought, *Oh that's great.*

Frank said, "He's been talking about going to Columbia on some gold deal or something. I'd stay away from him."

"That won't be a problem," I said.

When I got back to the mine, I told Mike about what I saw at the Truro Mine and added, "I don't want to be any part of that. It's extremely dangerous. I'll try to get them a couple of CB radios so in case something happens, they can reach out. They could at least talk to the store or somewhere where they might be able to get some help down in there, but for me, I'm going to stay out of there. I'll fill the boss in when I talk to him the next time."

Mike told me, "I would sure like to meet Benny and Frank."

I said, "Yeah, that would be fun. Kup and some of his camp want to go down there to the river and go swimming. One of these afternoons on a weekend we'll go gather everybody up, and we'll go down and see Frank and Benny."

He said, "That does sound like a good time. How about next weekend? Diane's going to be out of town. I'll come over and spend the weekend at the mine."

"All right. I'll talk to Kup, and we'll see who wants to go."

The next morning, I was surprised by a visit. Tony and his son came up that morning. It was unusual for them to do that. When I met them, they said they wanted to talk to me about something that they had thought of. "What going on?" I asked.

Tony said, "When I shut this mine down in the 1940s, Ken, the man that was working here for me, was drilling straight down in the bottom of the mine on the right-hand side with a jackhammer. He was in a crevice, a big one. I want you to find that crevice. Now! Today! I want you to go clear to the bottom of it."

I looked at him with dismay. "Over on that side of the old pillar is just mud. We have never gone in there because it was an old working area, and I didn't think it was too safe. There is about a foot of mud in there."

He said, "Well, let's clean it out and see what it looks like."

So, I got the whole crew together, and we started digging the mud out of the mine. I couldn't believe it—we were shutting down everything else that was going good to dig in the mud. I looked at Mike while we were filling the mine cars.

He looked at me and just shook his head. "Not much pay in the mud," he said.

Denny gave him a bad look.

Tony hadn't heard him. I made a motion to shut up. He pays the bills.

After about three and a half hours digging in the mud, we found the crevice. It went down about two feet. It was about six feet long and two feet wide.

I looked at Tony and said, "Do you know what you're asking us to do, to sink a shaft in a tunnel? We will have to put up some high scaffolding. We will have to have a winch to winch the buckets out, and we'll have to timber the hell out of it if the top comes in. That's just our grave!"

He said, "Well, let's get the timbers; I'll get the scaffolding. We'll get an electric winch, and I'll have it all in here by next Monday."

I asked, "Are you sure you want to do this?"

About that time Denny said, "There might be more gold in the bottom of that crevice than we've got out of the whole mine so far."

Mike looked over at him and he said, "Do you know what a boil hole is?"

Denny said, "No."

Mike said, "That's a crevice that is tilted back against the flow of the water and all it does is boil when the water comes over it and gold does not go down in it. That's what that is. It is a boil hole!"

Denny looked at him and said, "I'll see you Monday."

After they left, Mike and I and the crew got together. I told them that they would not have to work in that hole, that Mike and I would take it to the bottom. I felt the same way as Mike did that it was a boil hole. We used to find them a lot when we were dredging in rivers with a dredge. Ninety percent of the time there was never, or hardly any, gold in them. But he was the boss and this was his mine, so we would do what he asked. I told them to go ahead and finish the rest of the week working in the tunnel. Then we would start that new project next Monday. John and Randy would cut timbers and clean up around the plant. I had a lot for them to do outside.

After Randy and John went home, Mike went over to his pickup and came back with a bottle of whiskey and said, "We might as well drink this before we die in that hole."

I said, "Mike we've done that before on the outside. We'll make it safe. I don't believe there will be a darn thing in the bottom of that hole. It's gonna take some time to get that thing dug out. I don't have an idea how far it'll go down. Just put the whiskey in the trailer. I don't want you drinking and driving on that road. I need you more than ever now.

He said, "Well, why don't you come to the Coach House and have dinner with Diana and me? We will get with Kup Saturday or Sunday and go down to the river to Frank and Benny's."

I said, "That sounds like a plan."

I was very unhappy. Everything had been going so well. We've been making enough pay so that we were making the payroll and fuel cost and above. Now we're going to shut down for who knows how long for a whim. In all the years I worked for that man, I never questioned him because he signed my checks, and I would do exactly what he told me to do even though sometimes I disagreed. I thought the world of him, but I didn't like what we were going to have to do. And if anything looked to me like it was going to be completely unsafe, I would shut down immediately. I didn't want somebody getting hurt and have that on my conscience.

I followed Mike out with my truck to go have dinner. We stopped at the Iowa Hill store and had a couple beers. We talked to Moe, and he said he was going to have some entertainment for the holidays.

I asked him, "What kind of entertainment?"

He said, "I have some Sumo wrestlers visiting from Hawaii that play ukuleles, and we'll have a dance."

Mike started laughing and said, "Well, we'll have to gather up every female on the hill to have a full set of teeth."

I hit him in the side. I apologized to Moe and drug Mike outside. He was still laughing when he got in his truck. I had my own vehicle. He followed me down the hill.

When we got down to the old bridge, crossing the river, I noticed on the bridge there was a woman in a red bikini and a man with long black hair hitting her in the face. He had her slammed up against the side of the bridge. I slammed on the brakes, got my shotgun, and got out of the truck. I ran up to him, grabbed him by the hair and pulled him off of her. She was bleeding profusely—her nose and around her face. I yelled back to Mike who pulled up behind me to get the first aid kit.

I asked her, "What's going on here?"

She couldn't talk. She just was crying.

When I turned around, the dude was walking away. I told him to stop, but he just kept on walking. He knew the sound that came next, the sound that comes when you pump a load of buckshot in the barrel of a shotgun. He turned around and walked back to me.

I couldn't help it. I hit him right in the face with the butt of the shotgun, and he went down. Now the woman beater had a nosebleed of his own. Bandit was trying to get out of the passenger side of the truck. He was tearing the door off on the right side. I walked over to the truck and got him to calm down. I came back and grabbed the guy by the shirt tail and told him I was taking him to the sheriff in Colfax.

I started back to my truck, dragging him with me, when she started yelling. "Please don't! Please don't! I love him! He's my boyfriend. We just had a fight." I turned around and looked at her with Band-Aids all over her face.

I said, "Are you kidding me? This son of a bitch just tore your face up, and you want me to leave him here?"

She said, "Yes, please don't take him."

I turned around to Mike and said, "Can you believe this?"

He said, "It looks like a homeless camp over there. There's so many of them by the river."

I was getting in my truck looking at my door—claw marks and slobber all over the window. I was asking myself, *Why did I even leave the mine?* Then I yelled over to Mike, "I'm going back to the mine, you go ahead and have a wonderful dinner."

He said, "Are you sure about that?"

"Yup, I'm sure!" I backed off the bridge, turned the truck around, and started back to the mine. I stopped at the store, went in, laid my shotgun on the bar, drank four more beers, paid my tab, and left. I woke up the next morning with Mike pounding on my door.

He kept saying, "Get up! Get up! It's time to get up!"

I raised my head. It felt like somebody had hit me with a 2 x 4. I let him in.

The first thing he said was, "Who drank half my bottle of whiskey?"

"I guess it was me or the dog," I said while holding my head.

"Yeah, right. You gonna be okay?" he asked.

I said, "Yeah. Give me ten minutes to get dressed."

"What did you do last night?" he asked.

"It's obvious, isn't it? I had a party with a dog." I stumbled and threw up a couple times.

We spent the rest of the day cutting timbers and measuring inside the tunnel, making wedges to put on the top of the timbers and trying to diagram on paper what we would have to do to put this together to make this work. We spent the rest of the time cleaning out the pond with the dragline, dozing up some more material with a D8 cat, and cleaning up around the tail pulleys on the plant. We would be all ready for them when they came on Monday.

Mike would be coming back in the morning, and we would be going down into Kup's camp. Mike came in about 10 o'clock on Saturday morning and brought with him three huge boxes of donuts and told me he was taking them with us.

I told him I think they like beer better than donuts, but that was a good idea. We spent the next two or three hours going over things that we would have to do in the tunnel on Monday. I wanted to make sure that Mike and I were on the same page when the boss came in.

Mike and I took my pickup, and we headed to Kup's camp. The kids loved the donuts; they didn't last long. We spent a couple hours just talking to everybody. Everyone was friendly. Mike got a kick out of it when they kept calling me Hawk Kup. He laughed every time. He said it sounded like hiccup!

I asked how many wanted to go down to the river. Fred's two daughters, a boyfriend of one of them, Kup, and Little Kup said they would come. Mike and I took off for the river to the Truro with them all in the back of the truck. When we went by the mine, there was more equipment but nobody was there so we kept going right on down to Benny and Frank's.

When we got there, I introduced Mike and Kup to the older brothers. The kids took off for the river. Kup told Frank that they were neighbors and if they ever needed anything to come look him up, and he would help them. I think it took a load off their minds because they heard so many bad things about Kup that were not true, but that didn't apply to the rest of the dangerous people that lived up in the area.

It was starting to get dark so I blew the horn on the truck to get the kids to come up from the river. Everybody loaded up into the truck, and I noticed the one girl that shot the cap off the beer bottle was soaking wet.

"I don't have a towel," I told her.

She said, "That's okay. I'm just tired of being dirty."

That really stuck with me. She was a very cute girl. I could not imagine what it was like to grow up in that camp. On the way out, I ran into Charles. He was surprised to see everyone in my truck.

I told him, "We've been down to see Benny and Frank." He looked a little upset, so I assured him, "Don't worry about nothing. These people won't take anything from me, and they sure as hell won't take anything from you." Then I asked, "Where have you been?"

"Up at my house," he said. "I have a house up on the hill above the store, and my brother has one across from the store. We're going to start driving tunnel next week."

"Are you going to drive it where I put the flags?" I asked.

He said, "No. I have a man that told me to go another direction."

"Really? Well good luck!"

Once we got ready to go, he added, "I don't want a lot of people coming down in here."

I said, "Charles, if I want to come down and see Benny and Frank, I'm coming down to see Benny and Frank. If you have a problem with that, talk to Tony. And by the way, you haven't paid me for the two radios I gave you."

"I'll take care of that," he said.

CHAPTER NINETEEN

I took everybody back to camp. When I started to leave, I told the little girl, "If you want to earn some extra money, I'll have a little part-time job for you once in a while. You have to ask your parents, and if they say it's all right with them, you can make a few bucks to buy some new clothes or something. Let me know." We headed back to the mine.

Mike informed me, "I brought in an old spring bed, a single that folds up. I'll set it up in our shed, and I brought my sleeping bag.

"That's fine," I said.

"Do you want to drink the rest of the whiskey?" he offered.

"Absolutely not!" I was in no mood for that scene again.

We fixed a little dinner, built a fire in our firepit, and had a beer but no whiskey. The boss would be coming up the next morning with all of the equipment that he had promised.

I had asked Mike to get up early and have coffee made. Bandit woke us up about 5 o'clock in the morning growling.

I told Mike, "Must be somebody out there or maybe an animal."

Mike got up, got his rifle and a light, and went out and looked around with the dog but didn't see anything. He came back, and I had some coffee on by then, so we just stayed up.

Tony and Denny showed up about 11 o'clock with a load of scaffolding and an electric winch. We went in and started putting things together. By four in the afternoon, we had it ready to go. Denny took some tools back with him that we didn't need. He brought up some parts for the plant and a smaller drill to use in the shaft. We told him we'd get started in the morning and he made sure to let us know that they would be back up the next Friday.

Mike couldn't help himself and spouted off with, "You won't have to bring any buckets unless you want to take back mud."

I could tell that didn't go over very well.

Monday morning, we went into the tunnel and marked off a 5 x 5-foot square right over the crevice. That's how big the shaft would be going down to give us some room to work in it. It took us about two and a half hours to drill all the holes.

Then we went down to the powder magazine and just got stick powder 40%. It would fit in smaller holes better. We put the fuses in, put the detonating cord on it and shot it. After the smoke cleared, we went back in.

The blast had loosened some of the timbers, so we had to get a ladder and a sledgehammer and pound some of the wedges in harder. I was happy with it. At least the whole thing didn't fall down. We dug for the rest of the day to get things started. We went down about three and a half feet. We would have to drill again.

The next morning, we did the same thing. We drilled all the holes, loaded them, and shot again. Now we were down about six feet. I knew we could go down as long as we could shovel out of the hole but, eventually, we would have to start using the winch and the bucket.

The crevice didn't look like it was getting any smaller. We cleared around the top of the hole and put some heavy timbers all the way around it. We would timber now all the way to the bottom. We ran track right up alongside of it so we could dump the bucket into a car to take it outside. We piled up all we could inside. It looked like shale rock sitting on an angle—soft and brittle, fine grain and easily eroded with a lot of cracks in it. It would be dangerous if not heavily timbered. Doing that would take a lot of time and work to set everything in place perfectly to take the load so it wouldn't cave in.

By Friday, we were down about ten feet and had already burned up the winch. They would have to come up with something better than that. When Denny showed up with the checks and found out what happened, he was mad.

I let him know, "I told you that those winches wouldn't work. Those things are for pulling the car on a trailer. We need an air winch."

He said, "I'll go get one now."

"You'll probably have to go to Auburn," I said. "I don't think there will be anything like that in Colfax."

Everybody went home. He never came back that night. It wasn't until 10 o'clock the next morning that he arrived with the same kind of winch and put it on. He said, "This one's a little bigger. I think there was a problem with the other one, so they gave me credit for it."

I asked, "Where did you get it?"

"I got it in Vallejo," he informed me before he left.

That night, we got a good storm. It rained all night and was raining the next morning, so we shut the mine down. I told the guys I would get a hold of them when it quit raining. It was getting close to Christmas, and I was sick and tired of digging in that hole. I was glad to see it fill up with water from the rain. We would have to wait until it dried up and I could pump it out to get started again. I went out and called the boss and told him what was going on.

He said, "Well, just send the guys home. We'll start up after the first of the year."

I said, "That's great, but they do have some checks coming."

He let me know, "I'll send them up to Mike's house. You stay in the mine; I don't want anything stolen out of there."

I agreed and wished him a Merry Christmas. I was thinking *I got news for him.* I would go out Christmas Eve to spend Christmas with my mom. The kids would be over to their other grandparents in Auburn, and I had some gifts for them.

The next day, it was still raining, and Mike came in and said, "Aren't you going to the party?"

I inquired about the party, and he reminded me it was the one with the Hawaiians which I had forgotten all about.

"Come on," he said. "Let's go up to Moe's and see what time it's gonna happen."

We got in the truck and went on up to the store. When we went in, I noticed there were no lights. I asked Moe, "What's going on?"

He said, "I'm just sick. The electricity is down. The party is tonight. Without electricity, we can't have a party, and I bought food and extra stuff for tonight. Everybody's coming."

Mike said, "Let's go get our generator, and we'll bring it back here." About an hour later, we set it up next to the window outside the building and ran the cord through the window.

Mike said, "They can fire up their instruments, and we'll bring some lights."

I started laughing. "Why not?" We went back down to the mine and got the lights. I told Moe, "It's gonna cost you some free beer."

He said, "Free beer for you all night!"

About that time, the Hawaiians showed up. They were big Sumo wrestlers. I couldn't believe it. They were cool guys. They brought their instruments. Everybody on the hill we could pack in there showed up. We had a blast.

Early, about three in the next morning, we took everything back to the mine, got in the trailer, built a fire, and laughed almost the rest of the night until we finally crashed and went to sleep.

The next morning, it was spitting snow. I told Mike that I would meet him at Dingus McGee's Restaurant in Colfax and buy him dinner and bring the checks for the guys so they would have some money for Christmas.

He said, "All right. What are you going to do?"

"I'm gonna pull out of here Christmas Eve and spend two days with my mom and kids. I'll see you at Dingus McGee's tonight."

I went out that evening. Mike and Diane got there just before I did. We had a wonderful dinner. We visited, had a couple of drinks, and I started back into the mine.

I went inside my trailer and sat down, and a loneliness hit me that I never felt before. I thought about my time on the hill and the people here and all of a sudden, my heart was going out to them. I was the same as them—broken, lost, hurt, lonely and brokenhearted. These people have been my friends. They never judged me. I would never judge them. Kup said I was family.

Every time I would go up to the store, Moe would tell me how someday he would love to retire and have a patio boat. That was his dream. Randy, bless his heart, was just starting out in life. John was trying to find his life. Mike and I were both messed up.

Mike, my old friend that I loved, was the type of person that thought, "One beer—all boy. Two beers—half a boy. Three beers—no boy at all, Katie bar the door."

We both had been drinking way too much. I hadn't been taking care of myself. I couldn't even tell you what I was eating or cooking. I don't even remember. All I knew was there were people up here from all walks of life— good, bad, and ugly, and they were my friends. I thought about it, and tears rolled down my cheeks.

There was nothing for me to do tomorrow. It was miserable and raining. I thought *I'm gonna go down and visit my friends.* What lesson was God trying to teach me? I worked hard all my life and had never been in serious trouble. I paid my bills and took care of whoever I was responsible for. Why, for some reason, my Boss, after all these years, would think to open up this mine, and why all of a sudden did I fall into that spot? I didn't want my marriage to fail, and I missed my kids. I had a good job, a good home, and now I'm sitting here with tears rolling down my face, wanting to drink a bottle of whiskey. There were dirty clothes to wash, a dirty trailer to clean up. I was really on the pity potty of life and there was no place to go.

I looked over at my German Shepherd, Bandit. He was looking at me like, "You still got me, Dad."

I thought, *Yeah I saved you; they were gonna put you to sleep. Maybe that'll be the answer for me!* And I started laughing. I got my gun and said, "Come on, Bandit. Let's go for a walk." So, we spent the next hour and a half walking all over that backcountry. My head was starting to clear up. I told my dog, "We are all a bunch of misfits; we need to stick together."

After our walk, I opened up a whole can of dog food for him and gave him a bath. I told him, "I'm gonna buy you a new collar for Christmas. That one looks pretty ugly."

I cleaned up my trailer and put the dirty clothes in a bag. I would have to take them out to my mom's to have them washed. I built a fire. And we just sat around, me and the dog, two more days until Christmas.

Jim Bean

CHAPTER TWENTY

The next day, I cleaned out my truck, locked things up, put Bandit in the front seat and started down to Kup's camp. Everybody was there when I arrived. I noticed there was a lot more people there that I didn't know and some small kids. They were happy to see me. Kup came out to meet me.

He said, "Hi, Hawk. How are you doing?"

I said, "I'm all right."

"Come on in," he offered.

That was the first time I ever walked into that house. I was surprised it was clean and well-kept inside. Pappy Kup, Tom

Tom, and Little Kup were in the house with some other guys I had never seen before. They introduced me to them, and I walked over and sat down.

I looked down at the floor. They had an old battery and a radio and some wires leading outside to an antenna. Kup said, "The little kids were listening to Christmas music, but the battery went dead. I wished we had a better battery. That's an old one out of my truck."

I thought for a moment then told him to come with me outside. I walked over to my truck, lifted the toolbox, and pulled out a brand spanking new heavy-duty battery that I had bought for my trailer. I said, "Take this in. You can have it so those kids can listen to Christmas music."

He put his arms around me and gave me a hug, but this time he didn't break a rib. I spent the rest of the day and into the evening listening to their stories.

Kup told me how his life changed in Los Angeles and why he went to prison. He explained which prison he had been in and where he met Feather.

As I looked around the room, I wondered how many of them were running from the law now and were dangerous. But for some reason, I wasn't worried about myself. I gave up on that. I didn't care what happened to me anymore. I was in a dark place again, so I fit right in with the people on the hill. They trusted me. Their secrets for my secrets. I respected all of them. I thought, *These are all somebody's brother, somebody's father, somebody's son. They all went through life and made some bad choices that put them there.*

I got in the truck and went back to the mine. I would try to get down and see Benny and Frank tomorrow, Christmas Eve, before I went out.

The next morning, I had a bowl of cereal and a beer. I was going to leave after I saw Benny and Frank to go to Auburn but for some reason, I just could not make myself get in the truck and go. Then I thought about all the rain we had and that road going into the Truro Mine would probably be nothing but mud, and I might be able to get in there, but I wouldn't be able to get out. I just stayed in the trailer for the rest of the day. I was thinking it would probably be just a miserable Christmas and maybe I should just stay in the mine.

I lay down and fell asleep and woke up at 9 o'clock in the evening. I got to thinking my mom would think something happened to me so I had better go out. I got my things, the bag of dirty clothes, got in my truck, and started up toward the store.

As I went by the store, I noticed something sitting on the bench in front of the store. It looked like a little kid. I stopped and backed up and looked. It was a little boy sitting in front of the store. It was real dark that night, and there was nobody at the store. It was closed for the holiday. I got out of the pickup and walked over to him and asked him what he was doing.

"Where's your dad?"

"I don't know," he said.

"Where's your mom?" I asked.

"She's in jail," he answered.

"What are you doing here?"

"They kicked me out of the camp I was in," he explained.

"Why?"

"Because I stole something. You don't steal from people in the camp so they told me to go. I had to leave my puppy down there," and he started to cry.

"Your puppy?"

He said, "Yeah, my dog. I gotta go get my dog."

"Where is he?" I asked.

He told me approximately where the camp was. There was a little road going in there. I knew where it was. I told him to get into the truck. I turned around and headed back up the hill, down to where that road went down to a different camp. After a couple hundred yards, I pulled over and stopped.

"How far is it now?" I asked.

"Not very far," he said.

I said, "Go get your dog, and I'll stay here and wait for you."

"Okay," he said, and he took off running down the road. I turned the lights out on the truck and thought, *What am I gonna do now?* I was starting to get very nervous when I noticed him running up the road toward the truck with a little brown dog in his arms. He came up and opened the door and got in with Bandit and me.

"Where do you think you're gonna go?" I asked him.

"I have a place to stay in Colfax if I can get there. They'll let me sleep in the garage."

"Do you want me to take you there?" I asked.

He said, "That would be wonderful, mister."

I said, "Just call me Jim."

He said, "Okay."

As we started down the hill across the bridge and started up the other side, my heart was breaking. I never felt like this before. *Poor little guy. Maybe I should take him to the sheriff's department.* Then I thought, *No, I'll just take him where he wants to go.*

When we got into Colfax, he gave me directions to a house up on a hill. I pulled in the driveway. I gave him all the money in my wallet. He got out of the truck. I watched him as he went up to the house and knocked on the door. The next thing they did was raise the garage door. That would be the last time I would ever see him. That scene would break my heart every Christmas for the rest of my life, just to think about if he made it, if he had a life, if he was okay—that little boy from the hill.

When I got to Auburn, I was a real mess. My mom took one look at me and said, "Are you okay?"

Harry, her live-in friend was a nurse and said, "I think he's having a heart attack. We probably oughta take him over to the hospital."

I said, "I'm okay. I just need to go to bed." So, I did.

I didn't get much sleep that night. The next morning, I took a good hot shower. Mom made some breakfast that made me feel a lot better. I enjoyed the rest of the weekend. I got to see the kids for about two hours.

On Monday morning, I headed back to the mine with turkey leftovers and a half of an apple pie. I stopped and picked up some groceries and some books. It would give me something to do—some reading and some resting. I had to try to get myself back together before we started up after the first of the new year.

I spent that whole week just doing things I wanted to do. I went up to the store a couple of times and talked to Moe. I played some pool, worked around my trailer, cut some wood. I drove around and looked at some of the country, picked up some pinecones for my mom. I made one trip to Forest Hill for lunch. Now I was feeling a lot better. I was not drinking any beer, and I was trying to eat better.

Monday morning came, and everybody came into the mine. They were ready to go to work, and they were broke. They owed more money to the country store than they probably would make all week. The first thing we did was move things away from the tunnel entrance and start the pumps. It would take all day to pump out two-week's worth of rain that ran into the tunnel entrance plus what drained out of the ceiling inside. We would have to drain out the shaft that we were digging. That would take two or three days. Nobody was ready to dig in that hole, but we knew we had to.

We started in one morning drilling in the bottom of that hole. We put in some more timbers. I noticed that one of them had moved, and there was a crack in the side of the bank, so we added some wedges, and I put a steel jack in there. We shot that round, mucked it out, drilled and shot another round. Now we were down about 12 or 13 feet. You could hear the timbers pop once in a while. It was starting to make a lot of noise.

It took a lot of guts to climb down, and we went on down. I kept putting in more and more timbers and lagging up the sides of the shaft to keep the dirt from falling in. The hole was getting smaller and smaller. We were about a 4 x 4 hole. It was terrible, and there was room for only one man to work. Then we burned up another winch. I couldn't believe it. We couldn't do anything now.

"Mike, go get the jack leg," I instructed. "Go down in the tunnel and shoot a round in there. We'll start up the plant until I get a hold of Tony. I'll go out to Colfax and call him now."

He said, "I'll do that; I'll get John to watch my back."

Before leaving, I told Randy to work around the plant and get it ready to go.

I went up to Colfax and called my boss. "We burned up another winch," I told him. "I'm starting the plant up. I'm going to shoot a shot in the tunnel until you can get me another winch."

He said, "I'll send Denny up with one."

"The sooner, the better," I said. "We are almost to the bottom so you might want Denny to stay up here in your trailer so he can see what's in the bottom when we get there." He agreed.

I went back over to the mine. Mike was done drilling the holes, so we loaded them and shot them. We would muck that round out and drill another round while we were waiting for Denny to come up to get his million-dollars-worth of gold in the bottom of that hole.

That afternoon, two guys came into the mine dressed in camouflage. I told Mike to go stay in my trailer where my shotgun was until I found out who these guys were. They told me they were on the other side of the ridge, that they had a claim over there.

I asked them, "Why'd you come over here? This is private property." About that time, Bandit went completely crazy. I had to grab him and hold him. "I think you better leave before the dog breaks his leash and eats you up." I didn't like the looks of them anyway.

They looked at me and one said, "Really? There are two of us and one of you. We aren't afraid of your dog."

Then Mike stepped out of the trailer with my shotgun in his hand.

I said, "Yeah, really!"

They left and never came back, but I could hear automatic weapons over where they were once in a while. They would shoot over the ridge. Later on, I found out who they were and that was the end of that.

Two days later, Denny showed up with a brand-new winch just like the one we burned up. I told him, "That'll probably last until we get to the bottom because we're almost there."

We hooked it up and he told me, "Shut the plant down and quit drilling in the tunnel."

I said, "The only reason I was doing that was so you would have extra pay. "

"Go in the hole," he instructed.

I said, "It's your mine, and you pay the bills." We drilled another round in the bottom, tried out the new winch, and got down another four feet. I knew then we were only within a couple of feet of hitting the bottom, and I wasn't seeing any color in the gravel.

I told Denny, "We will hit the bottom tomorrow. Did you bring a camera?"

"Yeah," he said.

I informed him, "You'll be the first one on the bottom of the hole tomorrow after we muck it out to see what's in there."

He said, "That sounds great." He went outside into his dad's trailer.

I turned around and looked at Mike. He said, "I was right; it's a boil hole. There's nothing in it."

I said, "I don't see nothing. We got another foot or two to go."

The next morning, we drilled a short round. I got some half sticks out of the powder magazine, loaded them, and shot the little shot that put us into the bottom of the crevice.

I told Denny, "If you want to, you can muck it out."

He said, "No! You muck it out."

He didn't wanna go in the bottom of that hole, but he was going to take a picture of the bottom of it. I went down and cleaned it out. We dumped everything that came out of it in a special place outside on a tarp. I extended the ladder on down and told him to go ahead and take a picture to give to his dad, and then we'll go out and pan the rest of it.

He agreed to that. When he got down there, he found that there was nothing but the bottom of the crevice, not even a speck of gold in the bottom.

We went outside and ran the dirt that we brought out. Nothing—not a speck of gold. I thought of all of that time we wasted digging in that hole. I know it cost a fortune to get down there.

I said, "Well, what do you want to do now?"

He pointed his stubby finger at me and said, "Go in the tunnel and drill."

I told him, "It's almost quitting time. We are not drilling."

We got in a heated argument. He took off running toward his truck, and I took off after him. I was wearing rubber boots but kept right on his heels. He was faster than me and was able to jump in his truck. I was grabbing his shirt through the window trying to pull that little dude out of the truck, but I couldn't keep up and had to let go. He drove up on the ridge and looked down at us.

Mike said, "I guess you're fired, having a problem with the boss's son."

I muttered, "Yeah, probably, but that's okay. I'll find something to do somewhere."

He said, "What are we gonna do about the checks?"

"I'm going to Vallejo to see the old man," I assured him. "I'll bring them back tomorrow morning. You go ahead and start drilling in the morning and run that stuff we pushed up with a cat. I want the plant running."

He said, "All right. See you tomorrow, I hope."

Jim Bean

CHAPTER TWENTY-ONE

I went straight to Vallejo and went to Tony's house. I told him what had happened and I apologized for being angry.

He told me, "Sometimes people just aren't seasoned yet." He gave me the checks and said, "I'll be up next week."

I said, "See you then. We're gonna start running full blast."

"That's good," he said.

"I have a new area I want to go into," I informed him.

Everything went normal for the next three weeks, we drilled, shot, and moved ahead in the direction I wanted to go. It was good pay. We were *finally* making some good pay.

One afternoon after work, I was up at the store and when I pulled in. I noticed a green car with three guys sleeping in the back seat. One guy was in the front seat. They looked like they were all passed out or had been up all night. I walked into the bar, and the only person in there was Moe.

"What's going on?" I asked.

He pointed at the bathroom. I moved around against the wall and out came a woman with heavy make up on. She walked across the floor and back out to the car.

"I don't like the looks of that!" I told Moe.

He said, "I don't either."

"I'll get the license plate. You call the sheriff and get him on the line."

He said, "I can't; the line's down again."

"Then I'll stay here until they leave." They left and headed out. The route they took was the road that would go all the way around and come out by the dam and then into Forest Hill. I thought maybe that's where they were going.

Two days later, I ran into Kup, and he told me they were a bunch of dudes that stuck up a service station in Sacramento, and he ran them off the hill. Two nights later, Moe had somebody come into his driveway and stay there until he went out with his mini 14 and shot a half a clip full of shells in the air until they left. We never saw them again.

Kup told me that in the spring there are always a bunch that come in there wanting to stay, and he won't let them in his camp. Some of them were growing weed in the Manzanita patches and would water them by hand.

We were not to trust anybody. I remembered what the sheriff told me when I first got my blasting permit—the only way he would come in there would be with a S.W.A.T team, so with that said, I would be on my guard. We put a locked gate at the top of the hill coming into the mine.

One morning, I was coming into the mine from Colfax just above the bridge. I ran into a woman walking alongside the road. I had a foreman from the company down south with me. I told him, "Move over; we'll give her a ride."

That was a mistake. We could've been sitting in the front seat with Sasquatch. I asked her, "Who are you?"

She told me, "I live in the Tiltin' Hilton."

"No kidding? You're the girl that lives there?"

"Yes," she said.

"Why do you live down there?" I asked.

She said, "I was taken up by a flying saucer, and then I was put back down at that cabin. I went back and forth several times in the flying saucer, and each time, they would drop me off inside the cabin."

All I could say was, "Okay."

She said, "Drop me off at the trail above the store."

After we let her out, we rolled down all the windows in the truck.

The man who was with me from Vallejo wanted to go down into the Truro to see what was going on. Tony had sent him up there to see if he could help down there. I was glad for that because I didn't want anything to do with it.

On the way down in there, we came around the turn and there was a huge timber rattler in the road. I told him I was going to get out and shoot it. I got out of the truck. The rattler was going next to the edge of the road. I took a shot and hit him dead center, but he kept going. I went over to the edge of the road, and my feet went out from under me. The rattler and I both went over the steep bank.

I didn't know where he went. It didn't take me long to get back up on the road. When I got to the truck, the guy had locked all the doors and was looking straight ahead in a frozen state with a dead look in his eyes.

I hollered, "Open the door!"

He said, "I never saw a snake that big in my life!"

I repeated, "Open the damn door!"

He finally did after yelling at him for several minutes. After I slid into the truck, I asked, "What did you think the snake was gonna do? Open the door and come in and get you?" This guy was definitely a wimpy dude and would not last long on this hill.

When we arrived at the Truro Mine, Charles was unloading a huge dump truck tire, brand new, out of his truck. It was a tire with a wheel in it—real heavy. When he pulled it out, he couldn't hold it. It bounced twice then bounced over the bank. We could hear it bounce through the rocks and bushes. It went clear down into the American River. He stood and watched it go. I couldn't believe it.

I got out of the truck and said, "Well, that was a loss of about 350 bucks. What are you guys doing down here now?"

"We're driving tunnel," he said.

"Where?" I asked.

He showed me where they were driving tunnel in solid rock. They were in about 100 feet going the wrong direction from where I told them to go, where I had placed the stake in the ground. I dropped off the foreman that was scared of snakes and told him I was going down to see Benny and Frank and would pick him up on the way out.

Frank was sitting there with a gold pan in his hand with some nice nuggets in it. He said they got them that morning.

I asked, "How is the world treating you down here?"

He said, "It's awfully noisy, and I wish those guys weren't up there. Every time they blast, it shakes our whole cabin. We don't like it a bit."

I said, "I don't think it'll last long. If you guys need anything, let me know or tell them up at the store, and I'll bring it down to you."

I left and picked up the genius and took him back to his truck so he could go down and report to the old man how he was going to help them find the glory hole. After I dropped him off, I picked up some groceries and headed back into the mine.

CHAPTER TWENTY-TWO

Everything was going great; no problems whatsoever. We were having good cleanups, and the old man was happy and the kid was staying away except to bring checks up. With things going well and a gate up at the top of the hill, it would give me a chance to go out. I would sometimes go over to Mike's home and go to the Coach House Restaurant for dinner on Saturday nights.

I had my eye on a waitress there. She was a nice person. I had known her for quite some time, so I asked her out for a date. I only had to go out one time to find out that she had been married three times to three different cops. All the furniture in her house was white—the place looked like a hospital. That was the last time I pursued that. After that, I never talked to her again. I figured she had a lot of baggage, and I didn't want to be fourth in line.

One week later, Tony and his wife came up to the mine. They wanted me to ride up to Charles's house with them in his car. When we got just in front of the store, a guy with a shotgun was on the side of the road and pointed it at the windshield. I had a 357 in my pocket.

Tony stopped the car and about that time, another guy came out the door of the bar with a top hat on. He wore a long black coat. He was very unkempt and had a gavel in his hand. He pounded on top of Tony's car with the gavel. This situation looked very serious, and Tony's wife was getting upset.

He said he was a judge and they were raising money for somebody that was sick. I looked over, and I saw Moe with his legs over the cliff behind the store with two guys standing there with him. *What the hell was going on?* I thought I was going to have to shoot somebody. I got out of the vehicle, mad as could be expected.

Someone yelled that it was the Clampers—a club of men who dressed up like western cowboys but were just a bunch of sloppy drunks most of the time. They were bringing Moe into the club. They were initiating him and taking up an offering. The judge walked over and took the gavel and hit the top of my boss's car again. I stepped out the other side and drew down on the guy with a shotgun and told him if that gun he had was loaded and he pulled the trigger, he was gonna die.

Tony told me to calm down and told the judge that he was a contractor and gave them five dollars. I got back into the car, still looking at the guy with the shotgun and thinking how stupid that was as we drove up to Charles's house. I told Tony, "You don't know what you're going to run into up here. It's better not to say anything until you know what you're dealing with."

When we got up to Charles's house, they both talked about the Truro Mine for about an hour before we left. That's when I asked, "By the way, when are you gonna pay me for those two radios?"

He said, "Oh, I forgot. I'll come over next week with your money."

As we drove away, Tony asked me, "What radios?"

I said, "I put in two real good CB radios, a base station, and the other one is in his truck in case they have a problem so at least they can call for help to get out of that hole." I told Tony I didn't want anything to do with that down there."

He just said, "Well, we'll see." We went back to the mine, and they went home. It was uneventful.

Within the next few weeks, spring was coming. I couldn't wait for good weather. I brought the little gal over—the teenager from Kup's camp—and gave her some money to clean my trailer once a week. The only thing she wanted was to be able to use my shower. She couldn't stand being dirty. She was a good girl.

One weekend, her family invited us over for a barbecue. I told her we would go. It was going to be on a Saturday in the afternoon. I asked Mike, "Do you really want to drive all the way over there for a barbecue?"

He said, "Sure, I'll be there."

I said, "Come here first in case something changes."

He showed up Saturday morning and got something out of his truck. It looked like a beach ball. He said, "I wanna put this in the back of your truck."

"What is it?" I asked.

He said, "It's a boom boom."

"Mike, what is it?" I repeated.

He said, "I'll show you when we get over to the barbecue."

When we got down into the first camp where the family was, they had a barbecue going and there were quite a few people there. They made a great big circle in the dirt, and they had chairs around it and a few logs to sit on. There was a bunch of chickens walking around, a lot of dust—the place was filthy.

I asked what they were cooking. They said it was a black goat that had been walking around down at Kup's camp all winter. I walked over to the tables they had set up, and I looked in their pan and the meat looked real stringy. They also had a big pile of beans.

I looked over my shoulder, and Mike was showing this big round beach ball that he had to Kup. I walked over to see what they were talking about. They were both laughing and standing on the back side of the truck. They motioned for me to get behind the truck. There must've been 30 people in the circle sitting on the logs and chairs. I looked at the beach ball as it bounced in the middle of the circle, and it had a fuse on it; Mike had lit it and tossed it out into the circle where the chickens were.

After a short time, there was a huge explosion. I couldn't see anything but dust, and then saw a lot of feathers floating down from the air, when it cleared up a little. I could see that all the chairs, were flipped over and feet were sticking up behind the logs. Kup was laughing his brains out.

I asked, "Mike, what did you do?"

He said, "I filled the thing up with gas. It makes a good firecracker." Everything, including my truck, was covered with dust. I looked up at the barbecue and there was dust floating down everywhere.

Mike started laughing until I thought he was gonna collapse. There was not a chicken to be found when everybody started crawling up to pick up their chairs and sit back on the logs. I thought we were going to be killed. But instead of that, everybody broke into a big laugh. The chickens returned with large patches of feathers missing covered with dirt. Thank God nobody was hurt.

The barbecue pretty much was ruined so I said, "I'll take everybody up to the store to buy you hamburgers."

One of them said, "No, that's not necessary. We'll eat dinner anyway." We stayed there the rest of the afternoon laughing about all the crazy stuff and eating goat and dusty beans.

When we got ready to go home, Kup came over to us and said, "That was the funniest thing I've ever seen."

I told him, "I didn't know Mike was going to do that."

He said, "That's okay. I like Mike."

When we got back, I told Mike, "Don't ever do that again."

He just started laughing again. We sat around the fire that night until about two in the morning, drank a few beers, and did a lot of laughing. Mike said, "I'm going to be sad when this is over."

I said, "Are you kidding? I can't wait 'til it's over."

He said, "You don't really mean that."

I agreed. "No, I guess not. I'm happy where I'm at."

CHAPTER TWENTY-THREE

The next few weeks, it was mining as usual. We drove tunnel, brought out the ore, ran it through the plant, and Denny would come up and clean it up, and put it in buckets to take back to Vallejo.

I had been here on the hill long enough now. I pretty much knew everybody on the hill. Tony had me buying gold from some of the miner's that were up there. I was paying them above spot, so I got to know a lot of the other people that were mining here, too, that nobody knew about.

School was out in Napa, so I went down and picked up my son. He was 12 years old. I brought him up to the mine. He could stay with me for two or three weeks. I really enjoyed having him up there. After work, I would put him on the loader and teach him how to dump ore in the plant. He was a natural, and he loved going underground with me walking around and looking at things. He even found a piece of rock with a nugget in it. I gave it to him. He still has it today.

While he was there, I pretty much stayed away from everybody except our mine crew. Occasionally, I would go up to the store and buy him a hamburger, but that was it. Those three weeks were wonderful.

When he went home, I was really sad to see him go. It made me start to look at things differently and the way I've been treating myself. The things that I'd been doing weren't healthy for me. I thought about how much I missed just having a job and having a home to go back to at night.

I spent a lot of time after work walking around with the dog and occasionally driving around in the truck and looking at the country.

One afternoon, I stopped at the store, walked in and looked at Moe and saw that he was packing a gun on his hip.

"What's going on?"

He said, "There's some new people up here on the hill now, and I don't trust any of them."

"Really? Are they down in the hole?" I asked.

He said, "I don't know. I heard the Truro shut down."

I had not seen anybody, and nobody had told me that so I thought I'd drive up to Charles's place and ask him what was going on. I saw him standing out in front of his house. I drove up alongside of him. Bandit was in the back of the truck.

Charles was drunk as a skunk staggering around. I asked him what was going on. He said, "I shut the mine down. Ran out of money. Somebody broke into my house and stole the base station you gave me and some other things."

"That's too bad," I told him. "Is there anything I can do for you?" But he said he was okay.

I started to drive away and Bandit leaned over the side of the truck, hanging on by his toenails, with ferocious barking and growling like he wanted to chew his head off. The last thing I saw in my rearview mirror was Charles sitting on the ground looking at me as I drove away. That was the last time I would ever see him.

The next week was pretty rough. We didn't find anything, and we were running into the end of the property underground so I decided to back up and go out toward the entrance and start a new tunnel.

Tony and his family came up. He was concerned with the bad week. We had drilled two shots in the new hole, and I brought it out and started the cleanup. It was red hot. There was a lot of gold in it. I knew we didn't have much ore left in that one area, but it really looked good.

Tony and Denny panned that afternoon in an old tub that I had for them. My boss's wife decided she'd pan one pan, too. When nobody was looking, I dropped two half-ounce nuggets in her pan that we had found the week before. She smiled and acted like she had just found them. It was a good day.

The next three or four shots were the best we ever found, but it wouldn't last long because we would break into the other old tunnel and it was already worked out.

That weekend when everybody was gone, I decided to take a trip into Kup's camp. As I started down in there and got to where Fred and his family were normally, there were some people there I'd never seen before and one big guy that was just staring at me. I got out of the truck and asked where Kup was. They pointed over by the bank. I walked over, and he was shooting up with a needle in his arm. I couldn't believe it!

He said, "How you doing, Hawk?" I knew right then I needed to get out of there.

I said, "I just thought I'd stop by. I'm going out, and I wondered if you needed anything. If so, I'll bring it into you."

"I don't need anything," was his reply. "You want some of this?"

I said, "No, I'm fine. I'll see you later."

The big guy looked over at Kup, and I remember him asking who in the hell I was. Kup told him to, "Shut up."

I was in my truck and started out of there. I never saw the two young girls or that family ever again. About three days later, I was told that there was a big fight down there and that Little Kup had been stabbed in the liver with a knife and that Kup had beat the guy that did it pretty bad. They had taken Little Kup to Auburn Faith Hospital.

I left and went down to the hospital. I found out which room he was in and went in. There was a woman with him. She said that she was his mother. She was a very classy woman and looked very nice. She was probably in her 50s. She said she was from New York and that she was taking him back with her. I would never see him again.

When they took Little Kup to the hospital, Tom Tom was arrested because he had a pair of nunchucks in his back pocket, and now Kup was in trouble for being around him. His head was on the chopping block, too. He came into the mine that week and told me that he would have to prove that he didn't know that Tom Tom had the nunchucks when he was here and asked me if I could write a letter to confirm that he stayed out of trouble and that I had never seen him with any kind of weapons.

I told him I would write the letter because I never had any problems with him, but said, "This is the last time. You're on your own after this."

He said, "Okay," and left with the letter.

Things were unraveling on the hill. They would never be the same. About a week later, I was at my mom's house in Auburn and the phone rang. It was Feather.

She asked me, "Will you come in and get me? I'm leaving Kup. I want to go to my mom's house." Her mom lived in a trailer out past Bell Road.

"He'll kill me!" I told her.

"No, he won't. Come and get me," she said.

I drove back to Iowa Hill. I stopped at the store and got Moe's mini 14 rifle and started down to Kup's Camp. When I got there, nobody was there. All those people were gone. I stepped out of the truck with the rifle in my hand.

Kup stepped out and said, "You won't need that."

I put it back in the truck. I told him, "She called me and asked me to take her to her mom's house."

He said, "That's all right, Jim. Take her out of here."

She came out of the cabin with a suitcase and a big sack, it probably had extra clothes in it. I put it in the back of the truck, walked over, and gave him a big hug. "I'm sorry for all the things that's happened around here lately."

He said, "I'm glad that we've had a friendship; I'll never forget you."

We drove back up to the store, and I gave Moe his gun back. She never said much all the way out to her mom's house, and I didn't ask her personal questions.

When we got to the trailer, her mom came out. She seemed to be a really nice lady. I dropped her off and gave her a hug, knowing I would never see her again.

Jim Bean

CHAPTER TWENTY-FOUR

On the way back to the mine I was thinking about the last 18 months and all the things that I'd been through. I thought about all my friends and how things ended for them. I was starting to realize that life was pretty hard, and I would have to take another assessment of mine.

I was really sad. It was cold that night. I was lying in my dirty sleeping bag with the dog beside me thinking about everything. I couldn't sleep. I tried, but I just couldn't. Tears started rolling down my face. Something was going on within my body. I was shaking and crying at the same time. I looked up at the right side of my trailer where the big window was, and there was a cross in the sky. I just stared at it; I couldn't believe it. It was so beautiful.

I asked God, "If You're real, get me out of here. Please! Find me somebody that will love me, somebody that won't put up with anything that I do that's wrong." Then I said, "I would hope that she would be a brunette, nice looking, but mainly someone who will help me be a better person, someone who will come alongside of me for a better life." I knew God would have been laughing at my order. But at the time, it was real and I meant it for the first time in my life.

I must've fallen asleep. The next morning, I went out and started the pumps, fired up the compressor, and got everything ready for the men, but nobody showed up at 9 o'clock. I thought maybe the road caved in or maybe there was a wreck. *Where is everybody?* I wondered.

Then I heard a car coming down the hill. There was a man in the car that I had never seen before. He drove right up to me, got out of the car, and handed me a brown envelope and asked, "Are you Jim?"

I said, "Yes."

"You're the mine boss?"

"Yes," I repeated.

"This is for you." Then he got back in his car and left. I just watched him drive out, standing there with that brown envelope in my hand. I laid it in the chair by the fire pit. I went back over and shut everything down and came back and sat down in the chair and opened the envelope.

It read, *Cease and Desist. Shut everything down. Trucks will be on the way to haul everything out. Do not mine anymore.*

I could not believe what I was reading. I prayed last night for God to get me out of there, and the next morning I get a letter saying I would be out of there. The next line gave orders to go back to Vallejo after they got the equipment hauled out.

I couldn't believe it. There must be a God who answered my prayers. I would be going home and leaving this place about 4 o'clock that afternoon Mike came in said that the old man had called him and had already sent him up the checks to pay John and Randy off. He said there was a problem between the old man and his partners.

"I didn't know he had any partners," I said.

"Well," Mike stated, "obviously he does."

I said, "That's not my business. What do you want to do?

He said, "Well, I'm gonna have to find another job."

"I'm sure you can find one," I encouraged.

We spent the rest of the day pulling the shed away from my trailer. We spent the next two days pulling the big pipes out of the tunnel, taking out the mine cars.

One of the mine cars rolled over Bandit's foot in the tunnel when we were rolling them out. I had to leave and take him to the vet. They put him to sleep and sewed up his foot. I took him down to my mom's and came back up to mine the next day.

The trucks started coming in, loading equipment. In three days, everything was gone except the shed. Mike pushed up a big pile in the entrance of the old tunnel before the bulldozer left. Doc wanted the shed, so Mike gave it to him for two cases of beer. We were done.

I had a bad rash on my left ankle from wearing rubber boots. It was driving me nuts. I told Mike I would have to go to the doctor when I got back to Vallejo. I thanked him for everything, gave him a big hug, got in my truck, hooked up to my trailer, and followed Mike out.

I stopped at the top of the hill, walked over to the edge and looked down at the mine site for the last time. I had a strange feeling about what I was looking at and what I had witnessed. I would never forget my time in Iowa Hill. I felt like, for a small time, I went back into history.

I said a short prayer my way, for all those old minors that lived and died on that hill and that I had a chance to see what it was like, something that would live with me the rest of my life. I went by the store on my way out and shook Moe's hand and said goodbye. I hoped that someday he would get his patio boat. Then I turned around and went back out the other way pulling a trailer.

I would have to go back out through Forest Hill. When I got into the town of Forest Hill, my heart hurt, but I was happy to be going home. I didn't know at the time, but God wasn't through with me yet.

When I got down to Vallejo, I put my trailer in a trailer court and set it up. When I showed up at work Monday at the office, everyone was happy to see me and they had lots of questions. There were many handshakes and hugs.

Tony called me into his office and asked me when I wanted to go to work. That he had another adventure for me. I told him I needed to see a doctor about a bad rash on my leg but then I would like to get back to work. He told me to take whatever time I needed for that.

I made an appointment with a doctor that I knew well and after he examined me, he told me, "You need to see a dermatologist right now."

I said, "I don't know any dermatologist."

"There's one right down the hall. I will call him," he offered. "I'm sure they'll have to fit you in. I don't want you going home today until you see him."

I said, "Okay. I'll head down there."

When I got there, the first person I saw was the receptionist. She told me that I probably would be there for one to two hours and sent me into the waiting room. I sat down in the middle of the room, and after a short time, I happened to look over at the nurse's station. There was a really good-looking brunette looking right at me and smiling.

After about an hour and a half of looking back and forth with each other, I was called into the office. When I went by her, I asked her, "Why are you so good looking?"

I remember her laughing as she said, "I don't know."

When I got into the examination room. I never heard a word the doctor said. I just couldn't wait to get back out to see her again. She set me up with an appointment for next Tuesday.

I asked her, "Will you be here?"

She said, "Yes."

I said, "Well, I'll see you then."

After I left, I went over to a friend's house and was sitting there talking to him. Then I remembered, Tony said if I took care of everything, he wanted to show me something the next Tuesday.

Oh my gosh. So, I called the doctor's office, hoping she would answer the phone, and she did. I told her, "I will have to change my appointment."

After a few seconds, she said, "Well, that'll cost you."

I hung up on her.

My friend asked, "What did she say?"

"She said it'll cost me."

He said, "You darn fool! Call her back."

So, I did. I asked her, "What is it going to cost me?"

She said, "Lunch."

The next day, I met her across the street from the doctor's office, and we had lunch. After we spent about an hour together, we made a date for another time. Then I left, and she went back to work.

I remembered my prayer. Is that the girl God was sending me?

Six months later, we were married. I've been with her now 40 plus years, and we've had a wonderful marriage.

Did I go mining again? Yes, I did. I opened up an under-ground mine in North San Juan. After it was completed, the boss sold it. Then I went into open-pit mining. I worked 35 years for Tony and retired.

My 12-year-old son who learned how to run a loader in the mine, retired as number one loader operator at the Napa Quarry for the same company. He now lives in Nevada.

Sometimes at night, I think about those 18 months. Sometimes it's like a dream. I think about all the people. I know where one or two of them wound up, but I think about the ones that I never saw again. What kind of a life did they have, or what about the little boy that Christmas Eve? I still get a tear once in a while. But I know that the time spent there contributed a lot to how I changed my life for the better.

I went back one more time to see Benny and Frank down on the river. I took my wife, Kristina, with me. It was a wonderful day. They treated her like a princess.

Later on, I heard that Benny was coming down the trail to the cabin and, for some reason, he fell and landed in the forks of a tree, and they found him dead. I talked to one of Frank's relatives. He had moved to Forest Hill, and I know that he has passed away, too. God bless them all.

The first day arriving at the mine.

Breaking into the Chinese tunnel.

The main tunnel discovered. Pumping out the water.

Mike drilling.

Jim and Bandit in the main tunnel.

The plant in operation.

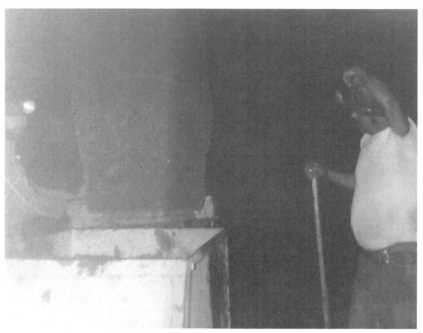

Jim and Mike mucking out a shot.

Mike using a mucking machine and dumping into a mine car.

Mike trying to remove the loud birds.

Jim's roommate, Bandit

Jim lighting fuses by hand with a Carbide light. (You can barely see the fuses.)

Mike pumping out an old tunnel.

Benny – Gold Miner

Frank and Benny's cabin

Frank, Benny's brother, on their mining claim on the American River

Powder truck

Sluice boxes.

Dragline cleaning out the pond.

Home sweet home.

Jim Bean

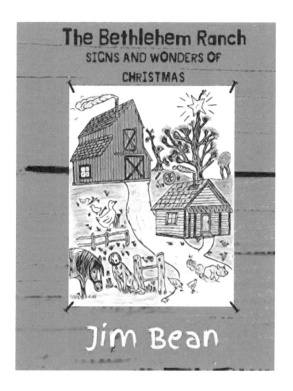

This is a fictional Christian story of a young couple who needed help on a stormy night several days before Christmas. The couple, Mary and Joseph, were expecting the birth of their child. With no place to go, they noticed a bright star and decided to travel to the light which led them to the Bethlehem Ranch. This creative story is about helping others in their time of need, sharing what you have even when there isn't much to share, giving love and joy to those who are alone and not gossiping or overthinking situations that you know nothing about. And it's about forgiveness and serving the best that you have and setting a place at the dinner table that looks like royalty for those who have nothing to give but the love of God.

Jim Bean

ABOUT THE AUTHOR

About the Author Jim Bean is married to Kristina Eby Bean (author of "Now That I'm Saved...What in the World are They Talking About!") with seven grandchildren.

Jim retired from Mining, Operating Engineers Local 3 when he was 55 in 1995. He was radically saved at a Revival Camp Tent meeting in Victor, Montana. They sold everything and moved to California, where they both graduated from Bible College and each became an ordained licensed minister in 1999. He was a Community Chaplain for Sacramento Law Enforcement, spent eight years in United in Christ Motorcycle Ministry working with outlaw gangs, and nine years working in prison ministry. He was asked to be, for a short time, associate pastor for World Inner Cities Ministries before moving to Idaho.

Currently, he is active in his home church, teaching. Jim is a cowboy at heart and has a deep love for the Lord, the old west, mining, and his bedtime storytelling.

Made in United States
Troutdale, OR
05/13/2024